THE SPLIT SCREEN STRATEGY

HOW TO TURN EDUCATION INTO
A SELF-IMPROVING SYSTEM

TED KOLDERIE

ISBN 13: 978-1-59298-855-6

Library of Congress Catalog Number: 2015947072

Printed in the United States of America

First Printing: 2015

20 19 18 17 16 15   6 5 4 3 2 1

Cover and interior design by James Monroe Design, LLC.

Beaver's Pond Press, Inc.
7108 Ohms Lane
Edina, MN 55439–2129
(952) 829-8818
www.BeaversPondPress.com

The e-book is available on the Amazon Kindle, Apple iBooks, and Barnes & Noble Nook.

To all those who have worked with Education|Evolving over the years.

Believers in paradigm change.

CONTENTS

PART THREE: IMPLEMENTING

PART FOUR: THE CHALLENGE

APPENDICES

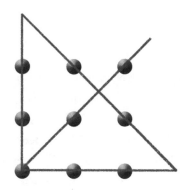

PREFACE

Hemmed In by Our Preconceptions . . . 'We Need To Try Different Routes to Solve Problems'

Many readers will recognize this graphic as the puzzle designed to test one's ability at problem-solving. You're asked to connect the nine dots with four straight lines.

Within the 'box' created by the nine dots it cannot be done.

Nobody said you couldn't run the lines outside the box.

This book is about applying that thinking to the problem in public education—where current strategy has long been caught 'inside the box', trying to reach the nation's objectives while remaining within the traditional concepts of system and school and within the traditional concept of system change.

After 30 years of trying, the suspicion is growing that it cannot be done.

But, again: Nobody said you couldn't find the solution 'outside the box'.

* * *

Paul MacCready and his *Gossamer* aircraft perhaps show us the way.

In 1959, Henry Kremer, a British industrialist, offered a prize of 5,000 pounds sterling for a successful human-powered flight. In 1976, Paul MacCready decided to try for it. He needed the money. He had built model airplanes as a boy; later, he flew sailplanes and rode hang gliders. In less than a year he won the prize when a man, pedaling, propelled his *Gossamer Condor* a mile around an oval course. Kremer doubled the prize for a flight across the English Channel. MacCready then built the *Gossamer Albatross* and in 1979 won that prize.

How did he do it when all the aeronautical experts had failed?

"Not having a background in structures was very helpful", MacCready told an interviewer. "All the groups that were serious about this project included aircraft structural designers. They adapted from standard techniques because that's what they knew and were comfortable with. Their planes were strong, and therefore heavy."

MacCready saw the obvious: that with only a single man aboard, flying 10 feet in the air and at 10 miles per hour, safety need not dictate design. He could build the aircraft to be light.

"When we tried to figure out why we succeeded when others didn't, it came down to a question of attitude. The Germans were thwarted by a prestigious professor of economics who gave talks on why the Kremer prize couldn't ever be won, and because they respect their professors over there, nobody tried."

For MacCready, the lesson extended beyond aeronautics. "There is little in our schools and our culture that forces us to get away from established patterns and to look at things in different ways . . . We need to be skeptical and try different routes to solve problems."

This book is about the need to be skeptical in thinking about the challenge of improving public education—and to be open to the 'different routes' that appear when we think outside the consensus.

PART ONE

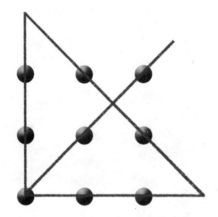

STRATEGIZING

The Problem

*"Alfred, your mother and I think it would be a good idea for you to knock about on your own for a while—**just on the estate**, of course."*

INTRODUCTION

Can Education Be Significantly Better
Without Having To Be Significantly Different?

So accustomed have we become to thinking a large problem must be a complex problem that it comes as a surprise to see someone writing about "getting to the heart [of problems] *where things are simple*".

Experience shows, however, that at their heart even large problems are often simple. What's centrally at issue in American education policy is simple. Issues are choices, and the choice confronting education policy is clear:

> *Can we be sure the effort to raise the skills and knowledge of young people will succeed with a strategy confined within, committed not to change, the traditional arrangements of system and school? Or not?*

Joe Graba, with Education|Evolving, puts it a bit differently; sets the issue as whether to approach the problems in education as problems of performance or as problems in the design of system and school.

In the 1980s, following the *Nation at Risk* report, there was briefly a discussion about 'restructuring' that implied the problem was in design. No clear concept emerged of what that meant, however, or what policy should do. So fairly quickly the consensus was to see the problems as problems of performance, and to address these by introducing the accountability model: standards, measurement and consequences. The conclusion, in effect, was that, yes, *school can be significantly better without it having to be significantly different.*

Several things made that appealing. Performance *was* a problem: Why not go after it directly? Also, a strategy that did not require disrupting the traditional system and traditional school was attractive politically. If while working to introduce accountability those shaping the strategy had proposed also to redesign system and school—to turn K–12 inside out and upside down—no one would have listened; not the educators and probably not the public, attached as it is to 'real school'.

Whether that decision was sound as well as convenient is another matter. After three decades of working to drive improvement into the existing K–12 system, none of the goals set has been reached. Appeals to 'stay the course', to try harder with the accountability model, are becoming less and less persuasive.

So the central issue is as alive now as it was 30 years ago.

What pass today for 'the issues' are not central. The disputes the media write about and that politicians fight about—as over testing, teacher evaluation and the Common Core—are second-order controversies generated by the decision to rely on the accountability model. It is time to go back to the central question whether the problem to be attacked truly is one of performance.

That consensus strategy is a risk

In a conversation with Mike Kirst some years ago, I wondered about that decision to improve 'performance' within existing arrangements. Mike thought a moment. "It is a one-bet strategy", he said.[1]

Several important concerns are now appearing about it.

Some have to do with its practicality. Will accountability be effective as the driver for improvement? Will the effort by conventional 'school reform' to make teachers accountable hold quality people in teaching—or will it drive them away? Is standardizing instruction the way to get all children to learn, given the differences among children? Can traditional

---

1. Kirst, for years professor in Stanford University's school of education, is currently again chair of the California State Board of Education.

whole-class instruction realize the potential of digital electronics? On and on.

One particular concern has to do with ethics. To bet all the chips on the strategy of improvement-only is a risk. It is not a necessary risk to be taking: Clearly, the country could be trying other approaches at the same time. Because it is not a necessary risk to be taking it is not an acceptable risk to be taking—with the country's future, and with other people's children.

The central issue urgently needs to be addressed. Does the country go on working only to improve performance in existing schools? Or should it be thinking whether problems of performance are created by system and school design? Is it time now to be trying some different arrangements of system and school?

Most important, perhaps, should the country be trying some different process of change?

It is time now to add an effort at *causing* improvement

The country should, yes, move beyond the one-bet strategy. That cannot be sufficient. There can never be enough time, enough money, enough political will and enough civic capacity to go on endlessly pushing into an inert system the changes and improvements that a successful system would be making itself, for itself.

There is no lack of concern about the problems, no lack of commitment to improve. Everywhere, individuals and organizations are trying almost to outdo each other in deploring the gaps in achievement and in reaffirming their commitment to do better.

Unfortunately, 'meaning well' and 'trying hard' do not move things ahead. With progress proving so disappointing, raising the level of concern mainly increases frustration. There has to be a 'how.'

It is time to be strategic.

Being strategic means doing what *causes* improvement; means introducing arrangements that drive (or induce) organizations to do improvements themselves; in their own interest, on their own initiative and from their own resources.

Shortly after leaving as CEO of Dayton-Hudson Corporation, William Andres accepted an assignment from Gov. Rudy Perpich to head a commission to improve productivity in Minnesota state government. Andres began by asking people: "Is productivity something you do, or something that happens when you do the fundamentals right?"

If you paused to think he would say: "I was in retailing. In retailing, turnover is very important. But every time a store manager tries to do turnover, profitability suffers. So we decided turnover is something that happens, and that we would concentrate on doing the fundamentals right."

Apply this now to education. If the idea is to act strategically—to cause change and improvement to happen—the question becomes: *What are those fundamentals to be got-right? Who specifically needs to do what specifically to get them introduced?*

The 'how' seems obvious

"Some things," a friend superbly skilled in public affairs used to say when he found people not understanding a problem or unable to see the way out, "are too obvious."

Were he with us today he would, I suspect, suggest the way out of this problem is to follow the common wisdom: When you don't know for sure what will work, try several different things.

With education that means getting beyond the one-bet strategy. It means doing improvement + innovation.

We often see two different efforts running in parallel. That should be possible in the effort to improve learning.

Surely it is good to keep on working to improve the schools we have. So, keep on with Common Core and accountability where states and districts want to do that.

Just recognize that improvement-only is half the strategy. Add innovation; open K–12 so new and different approaches to learning and new models of school can be tried. Give up the idea of a 'best way'. Do both improvement and innovation. Run the two side by side.

Think of it as a 'split screen' strategy.

Because it asks education policy to move outside its preconceptions, outside its traditional concept of school and also outside its traditional concept of system-change, that shift in thinking will be difficult for many in the education policy discussion.

It is important to understand why. So before proceeding further let's look at the way conventional thinking about system change blocks an effort to "get the fundamentals right"; impedes the effort to work simultaneously at improvement and at innovation.

CHAPTER 1

The Desire for 'Comprehensive' Action Is Blocking Change in Education

Many of those in the education policy discussion would like to go beyond incremental improvement within the framework of traditional system and school. They do want significant change; have strong convictions about the sort of change they believe is needed in system organization, in the approach to learning or in both.[2]

The concept of change, however, is of comprehensive change. Education policy seems driven by what Jal Mehta of Harvard so nicely calls "the allure of order".

The policy discussion is largely about whether the form of school and the approach to learning is right or not right. Proposals for change are advocated and debated pretty much as absolutes; arguments to go 'this way' countered by arguments saying 'No, *this* way'. Bob Schwartz urges the notion of 'multiple pathways', but his seems a lonely voice.

You can sense this dominent paradigm, the notion of a consensus 'right way,' implied in the talk about what 'we' must do, as in "We have to decide what students should know and be able to do". You can feel a desire for *the answer* in the fervent hope by policymakers and educators that research will reveal what is 'right'.

---

2. Even some state commissioners of education, frustrated, in private moments will exclaim: "We ought to blow it [the system] up and start over!"

Not for nothing was a principal history of American public education titled *The One Best System*.[3]

Some of the proposals for comprehensive change, some of those most controversial, come from persons outside mainline K-12. John Chubb and Terry Moe in 1975 pointed to political control as the problem and proposed a private market system. John Coons and Steve Sugarman designed a new system in making "the case for family choice". Milton Friedman argued for vouchers to permit parents to buy education in private school.

Those proposing to move away from the governmental bureau model of K-12 were resisted—successfully—by those inside. Inside, the appeal was mainly for loyal support and additional resources. But some within public education did propose a reconstruction of the system and of the approach to learning: Ted Sizer, John Goodlad, Albert Shanker, many others.

The *Nation At Risk* report was a call to comprehensive action—if without much clarity as to the action.

Education policy leans in favor of 'central authority'

Listen long enough to the discussion and you will sense how deeply rooted is the notion that, with consensus achieved, the 'right way' is then to be implemented with 'whole system reform'; that it must be 'systemic', with 'all elements aligned', and must come 'at scale'.

Underlying this impulse to find and to establish the one best system is what Professor Charles Lindblom of Yale University called the bias in favor of "mechanisms of central authority".

Explaining, in a talk at the Humphrey School of Public Affairs in March 1988, Lindblom said:

Most decision-making and planning proceeds through what I have called 'disjointed incrementalism'. Still, the human impulse is to try

---

3. David Tyack, professor at Stanford University, 1974.

to take control of complex situations. And essentially there are two models, or approaches, through which people try to act.

One is coordination and change through centralized decision-making. Here information flows from the outlying parts of the organization into its center and instructions flow back out.

The other is coordination and change through mutual adjustment. In this model, information flows between and among the independent entities. You must note that this is not 'decentralization', which still implies a center. In the process of coordination through mutual adjustment there is no center, no single organization.

Our traditional theory is that coordination and change necessarily involves and requires a central mechanism.

We all know real situations where coordination occurs without such a central mechanism. Yet there remains a powerful bias in favor of the idea of central control. Academics are trained to think centrally; to get a synoptic picture of 'the whole problem'. Consultants tend to take the same view. Comprehensive planners do, as well.

The process of mutual adjustment is messy and untidy and therefore unappealing to many persons. As a consequence, the most logical and intelligent people tend to underrate its potential.

This continues to be one of the major intellectual problems in the organization of human action.

Unhappily, 'changing everything' is not a realistic possibility

Our process of policymaking does not have a way to change everything at once. It cannot accomplish a comprehensive transformation from the existing system to something radically different.

A strategy of comprehensive transformation would require, first, the ability to develop a consensus on what is to be done, an agreement on the different model that is to be accepted as 'right'. Then, an ability to engineer a transformation of the system into that different model.

Reality eliminates the possibility of comprehensive change. 'A consensus on fundamental change' is a contradiction in terms.

Opinions and values differ too widely for anyone to assemble the majority required for political action on something radically different. Nor, were a consensus achieved, could it be implemented politically in our multi-state system with its commitment to local control. Radically different concepts of school challenge the public's notion of 'real school'. Different arrangements for school and for the teachers' role challenge boards, superintendents and unions.

Visibly, our political process does not engineer many comprehensive transformations.

Not surprisingly, then, policy fell back to the idea of doing improvement; to making limited, incremental adjustments within the traditional framework of system and school. Education policy seemed not to have a concept of changing *incrementally* the fundamentals of system and school.

That effort to 'improve performance' is likely to fail, as well

There was real hope the accountability model—standards, measurement and consequences—would work. On the surface it seemed reasonable, observing poor performance, to tell organizations and individuals to stop doing what is wrong and to start doing what is right. But the success of that effort seems now in question.

In the No Child Left Behind legislation Congress assigned the job of defining the standards and writing the assessments to the states. The states had a hard time resisting the impulse to set both at levels that would make their students appear proficient. The result was what came to be called a 'race to the bottom'.

That needed to be reversed, so an effort began to run, instead, a 'race to the top'. This involved pushing the states to install uniform standards, carefully described as 'common' rather than as 'national'; developed by consortia of the states. Fairly quickly the major state organizations were brought on board.

By 2014, however, serious resistance to the strategy was developing. Teachers and their unions were pushing back against testing, and among parents there was a growing inclination to 'opt out' of state standardized testing. It seemed increasingly apparent the 'consensus' was mainly among state and national officials. Some of whom are currently backtracking.

There is also, though less discussed, the possibility that the accountability strategy itself was flawed; might contain too casual an assumption that simply having standards will ensure student performance.[4]

Hope lives on that doubling-down on doing-improvement will work; that 'this time will be different'. But it is proving difficult to improve significantly enough and rapidly enough within the traditional givens.

In short: neither of the conventional notions of system change is likely to succeed: not comprehensive transformation and not the effort to improve performance within the traditional arrangements.

The problems are not what appear on the surface

It is easy for people inside and outside the K–12 institution to think the visible failures and misbehaviors are 'the problem'. The impulse then is to go directly at those 'problems'. For example, there are consultants who work with districts and schools on problems of student misbehavior, helping teachers improve their skills in classroom management.

Dealing with 'problems' in that sense is dealing with symptoms. We know from experience that the symptoms are not the problem; common wisdom warns against 'Band-Aid solutions'. Dealing successfully with

---

4. Go on one of the websites of the Common Core campaign and in the search box type the word 'ensure'; look at what comes up. In the business world, such assertions would be 'forward-looking statements' that a business corporation could not legally make without spelling out the risks that stand in the way of its strategy and its business plan succeeding. In the mail recently came a typical annual report—in which the discussion of 'risk factors' takes up 15 pages of the 10-K report.

problems requires getting to their causes. So, for example, a more effective way to deal with student misbehavior might be to make learning more engaging for the students.

At the end of a long discussion in New Jersey one participant, frustrated, said: "For an hour now we have been talking about all the bad things being done that ought not to be done, and about all the good things not being done that ought to be done. In all that time nobody has disagreed with any of it. And I'm willing to bet that everyone has heard it all before. What does that tell us? Surely there must be something causing the bad things to be done and keeping the good things from being done. Why don't we find what that is, and fix *that*?"

This is a known and successful approach. In thinking about France's growing concern about postwar Germany, Jean Monnet "had come to see that it was useless to make a frontal attack on problems, since they have not arisen by themselves but are the product of circumstances. Only by modifying the circumstances, 'lateral thinking', can one disperse the difficulties they create."[5]

It is what Bill Andres meant when he talked about improvement being "something that happens when you do the fundamentals right".

It is the strategy long argued by Walter McClure, of the Center for Policy Design: "Organizations and institutions tend to behave the way they're structured and rewarded to behave. If you don't like the way they're behaving, you probably ought to change the way they're structured and rewarded."

It would be well to take the same approach to the problem in public education. It is essential to get at the causes of problems. The causes lie in the arrangements of system and school; in the arrangements for learning; in the fundamentals.

So change does have to go to fundamentals. If that cannot be done 'comprehensively', substituting some wholly new and different arrangement of system or school, there will need to be a strategy, a theory of action, able to change the fundamentals incrementally.

---

5. *Memoirs*, Chapter 12.

Successful systems are those open to innovation

This country has systems that change that way; that are transformed, gradually. We are all familiar with these: communications . . . transportation . . . energy . . . information technology . . . medicine . . . the other systems with which most of us daily interact.

These are successful systems. While never perfect, they do raise quality and reduce cost; are responsive to their users; adjust and modernize as situations change and as the needs of our society change.

It is clear what makes these systems successful. They are, and are designed to be, open for the entry of even radically different ways of doing things. Individuals and organizations are free if they wish to step outside the traditional, to "be skeptical and try new approaches".

Public education has not been open in anything like that way. And it needs to be. *The fixation on comprehensive action is holding this country back from making the progress it could be making.* It is time to give that up. It is time for a different theory of action.

It should be possible to open K-12 to innovation so it will become, like these others, a self-improving system, a successful system that changes gradually but in its fundamentals. That would be innovation-based systemic reform.

After three decades of disappointment the burden of proof is no longer on ideas that have not been tried. The burden of proof is now on the ideas that *have* been tried.

This conclusion points the way, but does not get us there. We need to see how to redesign the system so schools and teachers will be able to innovate, able to try different forms of organization and different approaches to learning.

Let's move to that question next.

CHAPTER 2

Were It Open to Innovation, Education Would Change the Way Successful Systems Change

Systems do change without comprehensive action. Innovation spreading gradually is systemic change. It occurs when in "a collection of interacting parts" some critical element is altered and the other 'parts' adjust in response.[6]

Usually it is innovators who introduce the new elements that set in motion this process of system change. No consensus is required; simply the opportunity for the innovators to try their idea and for others to adopt the new and different if they choose.

This is not a process easy to establish or to maintain. Disruptive innovation is often resisted. The people proposing radical action are usually outside the mainline consensus; are often people of little reputation. "Invention"—the term Professor Lienhard prefers—is essentially an "act of rebellion", and rebels are not always welcomed.[7]

Often, however, those outside the established consensus see what those inside do not. And sometimes what results from their innovations changes the world.

- In the 1930s, waiting to have his cargo of cotton unloaded— bale by bale—from his truck and loaded—bale by bale—into the hold of a cargo ship, a small-time trucker named Malcolm

---

6. The way Paul Hill defined 'system' when at RAND Corporation
7. Lienhard was a professor of mechanical engineering at the University of Houston. See his *How Invention Begins*.

McLean wondered why it wouldn't be easier just to pick up his trailer and load that onto the ship. After 1945 he pursued that idea. Today 90 percent of the world's trade in manufactured goods moves in containers.

- One summer in the 1950s, a not-particularly-successful stockbroker looked at the regulation that blocked small savers from the higher interest rates available to those able to buy large-denomination bonds. He wondered what might happen if his firm bought large-denomination bonds and broke them into smaller units for sale to small savers. For some years, the idea struggled for acceptance. But today the industry of money-market mutual funds is in the order of 2.5 trillion dollars.

- Working at Motorola in the early 1970s, Marty Cooper had the idea of taking the early two-way radio out of the automobile and turning it into a truly portable telephone. He fought for a decade with company officials who wanted him to make a better carphone. But in 1983 Motorola put the first cellphone on the market. It weighed a pound and sold for $4,000. He kept working to get the size down, to get the price down. Today over half the people in the world carry cellphones.

Another, wonderful, example comes—curiously—from dermatology; from Mohs surgery.

In 1933 Frederic Mohs was a 23-year-old graduate medical student at the University of Wisconsin. At the time, the failure rate, the recurrence rate, for basal-cell and squamous-cell skin cancer was about 40 percent. Mohs worked out a way to 'fix' skin using a zinc chloride paste; then remove and examine a saucer-shaped piece of skin microscopically to see if the surgery did 'get it all'. The procedure could take a day or more. When a practicing physician, Mohs for a time had a motel in Madison where his patients would stay.

Surgeons took the view that dermatologists should not do surgery. But as the failure rate began to go down, Mohs surgery spread. And continued to improve. In the 1950s Mohs began to remove 'fresh tissue', fix it immediately and have the pathologist examine it. Today the patient might wait half an hour.

"I trained with Fred Mohs", my doctor said. I asked what the failure rate is today with these carcinomas, using this procedure.

"Under one percent", he said.

Successful systems change through innovation

Innovation, gradually spreading, is the way most successful systems change. Structured as open systems, they are *self*-improving; new designs and new models and new methods appearing; the organizations in these systems gradually adopting these changes—on their own initiative, in their own interest and from their own resources.

This country is not paralyzed by difficult, impassioned debates about whether all cars should be electric or hybrid, or whether everyone should use land-line phones or cellphones; fluorescent bulbs or LEDs. Change in these—successful—systems moves through the 'split screen' strategy.

Its essentials are clear.

The systems are open to innovation. It is possible for people and organizations to come into the field with new and even radically different product ideas and/or business models.

Early adopters pick up the new/different. Some always will be there at the start, no matter what the quality or how high the cost.

No one is compelled to move to the new/different. Those preferring the traditional may stay with the traditional. They simply may not suppress the different for those who do want that.

Never perfect when introduced, **the innovations spread, usually improving as they do.**

At the same time, **existing models are also improving**, sometimes picking up ideas from the innovations.

Over time, more people move to the new models. As they do, the whole system is gradually transformed.

In some industries and systems the transition is still under way or is only beginning: hybrid and electric vehicles are appearing, solar energy is developing, the incandescent light bulb is starting to dim out. In some, we can see a transformation completed. The world's last typewriter factory has closed; analog TV has been shut down, replaced by digital.

With innovation absent, the education system runs—and tolerates—an astonishingly high failure rate. It ought to be possible to do better. Among America's three million teachers there must be a good many Fred Mohs. We need to open the opportunity for them to show what they can do.

Innovation means challenging the givens of conventional school

Opening to innovation would mean creating an 'R&D sector' in which schools and teachers can try things. The R&D sector will be partly an organizational space; partly a climate of opinion open to and tolerating people doing-different.

The first step in applying that approach to education is to identify those elements in the current design that seem critical in shaping the behavior of districts and schools; those left unchallenged by the consensus strategy and that innovators might now challenge.

It is pretty much given that:

- **School is a place, a building**, to which children come at set times of day, week and year.

- **Attendance is compulsory**, usually to age 16. In practice, high school aims to keep students to age 18.

- **Achievement is still**—officially—pretty much defined as scoring well on tests of the "Three Rs": "readin', writin' and 'rithmetic".

- Students are sorted by age and move up the grades a year at a time, usually getting a different teacher each year.

- Standards are exit standards—with students expected, on graduation, to have mastered all major elements of the curriculum.

- The teacher is the worker on the job of learning. Adults 'deliver' education to young people, almost as if 'to learn' were a transitive verb.

- The technology is mainly whole-group instruction— students listening and working together in class-rooms; "batch processing", as Ted Sizer used to say.

- The school is not autonomous. It is a unit of the district, which is organized on the conventional public-bureau model.

- 'Professional issues' are reserved to management. Teaching is not a professional career, if 'being a professional' means being trusted to know how the job should be done.

- Teachers are employees working for an administrator. School has a single-leader model; the principal (presumed to be) both the instructional leader and the manager of school operations.

Challenging these givens will not be easy.

Education has not welcomed this concept of system change

The K-12 system is conspicuous in not having had a significant sector open to innovation.

John Goodlad put it bluntly in *A Place Called School* in 1985: "The cards are stacked against innovation". Its outside critics were equally blunt. "A backward industry" spending only a small fraction of one percent on research, development and evaluation, said a report as far back as October 1968 from a roundtable convened by the National League of Cities, the U.S. Conference of Mayors, the National Association of Counties, the Council of State Governments and the National Governors (Association).

Someone will of course point to districts and schools that depart from the traditional. And there is 'innovation' of this sort.[8] But a district's willingness to try one of almost anything urged upon it does not make that district a self-improving organization. Nor does such action by a number of districts make district public education a self-improving institution.

Often these different schools are a safety valve, relieving pressure from a particularly aggressive parent group. To avoid disruption districts often do not let these different models spread, even where demand exists. Districts sometimes point proudly to their waiting lists as evidence of their success.

Where change is constrained by state law or regulation, you might expect districts to ask the legislature to enlarge their ability to change. You might expect superintendents to say in public what they often say in private: that current arrangements are a problem. And might expect they would suggest it is the legislature's duty to act, having kept for itself the authority over system structure.

But they do not. "I have to work with the hand I'm dealt", I heard an exceptionally realistic superintendent say once: "the law, a board, teachers, a union contract, a budget, buildings, students, parents, public expectations. Reform means nothing to me."

In 1998 three leading Minnesota superintendents took an initiative to change "the hand I'm dealt"; moving to get greater flexibility for the districts: Don Helmstetter, that year president of the Minnesota Association of School Administrators (MASA); Jim Walker, a Minnesota 'superintendent of the year', and Tom Nelson, earlier commissioner of education.

In almost these words they said: With open enrollment, with standards and testing and chartering, the Legislature has created a radically

---

8. Though there is some tendency to exaggerate the change that does occur. In a conversation in the early 1980s the head of the superintendents' association in Minnesota was insisting: 'Education does too change!' Asked for an example he said: "Pregnancy leaves for teachers!"

new situation for district public education. We accept these changes. Now, in fairness, you need to give us the ability to compete in this new environment.

It is not considered appropriate for individual superintendents to approach the legislature for a change in general education law. So the three asked the associations to lead the change. Helmstetter tried at its annual meeting to get MASA to put their plan into its legislative initiative for 1989. Nelson took their proposal to the Minnesota School Boards Association. Both associations listened briefly and did nothing.

Education is not unique in its difficulty with change. Most institutions, most organizations, find it difficult-to-impossible to alter their core practices and values in truly fundamental ways.

Clayton Christensen has explained how powerfully internal culture and pressure from customers combine to constrain organizations from responding successfully when 'disruptive' new models appear as competition.[9]

Such change is bound to be harder still in the public sector. If business firms—operating in competitive markets and led by strong executives—cannot do more than make incremental improvements in their products and business models, who can realistically believe it will be easier—or possible—for governments operating in the political environment?

State leadership did in the '80s look for a different strategy

As the sense developed that America needed to improve the learning of its people, state policy leadership did begin to respond. By the 1980s it was common for a governor to want to be known as 'an education governor'.

Some of this took the form of improving financing. Some of it led in time to the effort to introduce standards. But some of it began to be about different arrangements and strategies in K-12.

---

9. Christensen, at Harvard Business School, followed *The Innovator's Dilemma* with a book about education: *Disrupting Class*.

Some of that interest in different arrangements looked toward delegating authority to schools. In the '80s the push for school-based decision-making came largely from principals. Bills were introduced; boards resisted. What passed, if anything, was enabling legislation; not much used. Still, the idea lived on.[10]

Some of it looked toward 'demonstrations'. As a legislator in Minnesota in 1973 Joe Graba helped create the Council on Quality Education— essentially a state foundation. It received good proposals. It made grants. The projects were successful. But 10 years later, as deputy commissioner, Graba helped shut the program down. It had become clear the projects did not last beyond the state financing and did not spread even within the same district.

A more strategic idea—ultimately more fruitful—appeared in the late 1960s from an obscure teacher/administrator in Massachusetts, Ray Budde. In a paper he titled *Education by Charter*, he argued for a two-level arrangement in which the board of education would essentially put its schools on contract and have the schools run by teachers.

The response? Zero. So he waited. In the 1980s the interest in 'restructuring' led him to try again, and in 1988 he got the paper reissued by the Northeast Regional Lab. One Sunday that summer his wife put down the paper and said, "Hey, Ray, you've made the *New York Times*".

In a talk in April 1988 at the National Press Club, the president of the American Federation of Teachers, Albert Shanker—as part of his effort to move teachers into professional roles—had cited Budde's idea and used his term 'charter' in suggesting that teachers be authorized to start small schools within schools.

The idea had consequences, as ideas often do. In Minnesota, a committee of the Citizens League took Shanker's proposal under study. In early October the Minneapolis Foundation brought Shanker to its Itasca Seminar, where the idea came to the attention of several legisla-

---

10. At one legislative hearing the school boards association, the superintendents' association and the two principals' associations all sat at the table in opposition. The head of MASA spoke for the group. This is a good idea, he said. But "we're not ready". Senator Janezich, a tavern owner on the Iron Range, looked at him and said: "Mr. Jensen, how old will I be when you're ready?"

tors. A month later the League issued its recommendation proposing the Minnesota Legislature establish a program of chartered (*sic*) schools.

In 1989 the legislators introduced the first bill. In 1991 chartering came into law in Minnesota.[11]

In the summer of 1990, with the idea in play, I had pulled the decade of policy discussion into a memo pointing to the 'exclusive franchise' as the central problem in system arrangements; had mailed the memo to people in education policy around the country.[12]

Quickly after 1991 it became clear the dynamics were right.

Governors and legislators, finding the districts were not giving them what they wanted, saw quickly that it was within their power to 'get somebody else who will', and to do that within the principles of public education.

At the national level, Will Marshall perceptively picked up the twin ideas of public-school choice and chartering and built these into the policy book that his Progressive Policy Institute and the Democratic Leadership Council were preparing for President-elect Bill Clinton.

Through the '90s, chartering spread rapidly through state legislation, establishing something of an R&D sector in public education.

What then happened—how far it succeeded and how far it did not, and what has become of chartering—is a story we now need to examine.

---

11. The story is told by its legislative champion, (then) Senator Ember Reichgott, in her definitive account of the origins of chartering. *See* www.ZeroChanceofPassage.org.)

12. *See* Appendix One for the key sections of the memo, "The States Will Have To Withdraw the Exclusive".

CHAPTER 3

Intended To Be an R&D Sector, Chartering Has Been Turned Away from Innovation

Chartering was an institutional innovation; a radical change in the K-12 arrangements, a step outside the dominant paradigm, creating a new sector of public education organized on a principle fundamentally different from that in the district sector and intended partly to generate innovation.

The laws that appeared around the nation in the 1990s did not create schools. Chartering was enabling legislation, opening the opportunity widely for people to create schools, and not specifying a kind of school to be created.

Despite efforts over the years to hobble it, the new sector has to some considerable extent functioned as an R&D sector. Unfortunately no clear picture of the innovation in the sector is available, because there has been no real study of the schools created.

As a result, few things in the education policy discussion are as misunderstood as chartering. Hopefully what follows will clarify on major points. The place to start is, as usual, at the beginning.

Chartering challenged the public-utility arrangement

Chartering has its roots in the frustration felt by governors and legislators wanting change and improvement but finding the K-12 system unresponsive.

K-12 *was* unresponsive. "This is a system that can take its customers for granted", Albert Shanker had said at the Itasca Seminar in 1988. Systems that can take their customers for granted can safely put their own interests first.

The question was what, practically, to do. In the mid-1980s governors and legislators were aware of the voucher option. But if they did not want to do that—and most did not—they believed they would have to do the best they could with the system in its traditional districted form.

Not so, it turned out.

Minnesota enacted the first chartering law in 1991. California acted in 1992, putting the idea in business nationally. In 1993 six states came in. By end of the '90s about 40 states had chartering in some form. What happened defied all political reality. These were 'state capitol policy initiatives', enacted with no real outside support and against the opposition of the associations representing the K-12 system, commonly regarded as the most powerful at the capitol.

As the legislation spread it began to evolve, largely in the direction of improvement. Even more striking was the way people began to create schools, in an astonishing outpouring of interest, commitment and effort.

The new sector differed in fundamental ways from the district sector. Four important elements are visible generally across the states and were present in at least the initial design.

- Innovation—There was no standard model of school prescribed. Broad-based waivers gave those organizing a school the flexibility to design whatever approach to teaching and learning they thought best and to shape the curriculum as they thought best.

- Accountability—Schools in the chartered sector were to be 'outcome-based' (the language of the initial Minnesota legislation), accountable to their authorizer for outcomes agreed with their authorizer; operating for a defined term of years with renewal subject to a showing of fiscal and educational success. This set a sharp contrast with the district sector, in which the schools owned by the district and run by the central office have no set term and in which accountability is bureaucratic and political.

- **Autonomy**—Autonomy and accountability are two sides of the coin. The idea was for the 'outcome-based' schools to be exempt from the laws and regulations applying to schools in the district sector, except for those that essentially define public education. The chartered sector was to avoid bureaucracy. Its schools were freestanding, single-unit schools, able to make their own decisions and to fix problems quickly when problems appeared.

- **Choice**—Enrollment was broadly open to students and was voluntary, on the theory that we do not assign people to innovations. Minnesota had introduced choice in 1988–89 as inter-district open enrollment. What was new was the idea of creating more schools for parents to choose among—and in some states the idea of designating entities other than districts to authorize these schools. Chartering thus opened opportunities for boards of education, and created new dynamics by removing the 'exclusive franchise' traditional in the public-utility arrangement.

The whole process represented the kind of 'national policymaking' that Conant had envisioned in proposing the creation of what became the Education Commission of the States: action nationwide, but not by the national government.[13]

It was an entirely appropriate action for state policy leadership to take. K-12 is the state's system; it exists in state law; dealing with its problems is the responsibility of state policy leadership. It was perfectly

---

13. *See* James B. Conant, *Shaping Educational Policy*; 1964.

reasonable for governors and legislatures, disappointed with the district sector, to get themselves a second sector designed to produce different and hopefully better results.

The charter concept is still fundamentally misunderstood

Though essentially a platform for innovation, a way to enlarge the system capacity for change, chartering is commonly perceived in terms of the schools produced. People talk about "charter schools". They evaluate the strategy by the number and character of its schools at the moment.

It is a serious misunderstanding to see 'the schools' rather than 'the strategy'. It is a mistake easily made, however, by those in the policy world who cannot understand innovation as a process for systemic change, locked as they are into the notion of 'comprehensive' change.

A second serious misunderstanding comes from the failure to look, carefully, to see what sorts of schools are in fact created. Education research paid little attention to the schools as schools; in general, seems not much interested in single cases of new and different. It is hardly surprising, as a result, that the schools created came to be known simply as 'charter schools'.[14]

As 'charter' became an adjective people began, predictably, to assume that a 'charter school' was pedagogically a kind of school. And that led people to ask: Are *they* are good schools? Are *they* better than district schools?

What followed was largely nonsense. Asking whether 'charter schools' are better than 'district schools' is like asking whether owned cars are better than leased cars—nobody looking to see what the cars are as cars or what the schools are as schools. It has been an embarrassment to education research; studies typically concluding that "the evidence

---

14. Describing schools is difficult-to-impossible, education lacking a taxonomy. There is a taxonomy for the animal kingdom and for botany; for geology and for chemistry. Education has no systematic way to describe and classify schools as the subject of its study. To see a design for a taxonomy of schools go to taxonomy.pbworks.com. Its author, Mark Van Ryzin, now teaches at the University of Oregon.

is mixed"—as of course it would be, schools differing so markedly one from another in each sector.

No student learns from a charter. Students learn from what their school has them reading, seeing, hearing and doing. To evaluate schools and their learning, research should look at particular schools to see what pedagogy is in use; then relate achievement to that.

Inevitably, too, the schools chartered were caught in the broader controversy about whether or not to keep and to expand the new second sector. The district sector did not quickly accept, even respect, the states' decision. As with many inventions, the appearance of a competitor aroused a strong defensive response.

Much research is essentially advocacy research, advancing one position or the other in the discussion. Advocates stress the virtues of choice. Opponents call the schools a threat to the districts; describe them in ways that make them sound as much as possible like voucher schools ("taxpayer financed but privately operated").

The outlines of the debate took shape early. About 10 years along, a change took place in the sector that both intensified and altered the debate. To understand chartering today it is essential to understand what occurred in 2003-2005.

New leadership took chartering in a new direction

During the first decade of chartering the schools and their state associations and support groups became loosely linked through the Charter Friends National Network (CFNN), created in Minnesota around 1996 with help from Challenge Foundation and others.

CFNN was not an organization; simply a project connecting the state-based organizations. Concurrently, at the Center for Education Reform in Washington, Jeanne Allen was keeping a nationwide inventory of the schools and the laws. There was no national organization charged to advocate broadly for the idea; to explain, defend and interpret it.

Around 2002 discussion began about creating a formal national entity to support and advance chartering through federal and state policy and through stronger state advocacy organizations.

What initially appeared in March 2003 was the National Charter School Alliance, a membership organization with a blend of state association people and national advocates to be elected to its governing board by the state-based membership. Howard Fuller, former superintendent in Milwaukee and founder of the Black Alliance for Educational Options, became its chair. Dean Millot, earlier with RAND and the New American Schools Development Corporation, became its executive and began to set up a Washington-based office and staff.

In the summer of 2003 several of the foundations active in financing new schools—including some that had supported CFNN—expressed a desire for a 'leadership organization' rather than a membership organization. This thinking crystallized at a donors' strategy session on July 17 in Charlottesville, Virginia, just prior to a meeting of charter actives called by the Progressive Policy Institute. It developed further at a second meeting in Philadelphia in early August.

The sense was, as one consultant put it privately, that for chartering to realize its potential "the little people" now needed to give way to "the heavy hitters".

The foundations withdrew the promises to finance the initial design. The National Charter School Alliance was dissolved. Staff were let go. Fuller appointed a group of board members to come up with a new design acceptable to the funders. That took another year.

In October 2004 the National Alliance for Public Charter Schools appeared as the Washington-based national leadership organization. Nelson Smith was brought in to be its executive. The foundation money then arrived.[15]

Over the next several years a number of state and local charter associations and support organizations—as in California and in Washington, DC—lost their financing. 'Strategic planning' grants became available

---

15. The name, the use of 'public' to modify 'charter', was unskillful. To make its point that public education now has a non-district as well as a district sector, the organization should have called itself the National Alliance for Charter Public Schools.

to those willing to fall in with the new initiative. By March 2008 most of the early state-based members were gone from the Alliance board.

With the leadership organization established, the next challenge was to establish a rationale and strategy for the reconceived chartered sector. This emerged from a task force created by the Alliance's new executive. Its January 2005 report was presented to a meeting of the charter family that Smith convened at Mackinac Island the following August.

Titled *Restoring the Compact*, the report aimed to establish chartering as about accountability for achievement conventionally defined. The strategy now is to attack the district system at what is seen to be its weakest point; its inability to produce schools that get elementary students in the inner cities to be proficient in English and math and to close schools that do not. The idea is to build the chartered sector by demonstrating that it can produce schools able to get students scoring high, and can close schools that do not.

On the 20th anniversary of the first chartered school opening, the Alliance, meeting in Minnesota, released *Fulfilling the Compact*. Later in 2012 the Progressive Policy Institute issued *Improving Charter School Accountability*.

Efforts focus on creating and 'scaling up' as quickly as possible a set of organizations—Charter Management Organizations (CMOs)—to operate networks of 'high-performing schools' and on closing 'failing schools'. More and more, the effort seems to be moving through the National Association of Charter School Authorizers (NACSA), an organization with broadly the same backers as the Alliance. In November 2012 NACSA announced a campaign aiming over the succeeding five years to close 1,000 'low-performing' schools and to open 3,000 'quality' schools serving one million students.

The effort is highly organized. A set of large foundations finances the key national organizations. Increasingly philanthropy in major cities is being organized in support. The reform effort has been able to broaden politically (Democrats for Education Reform), to draw in younger people (Students for Education Reform), to attract some in teaching (Association of American Educators, Educators4Excellence), and to appeal to those generally focused on higher standards and on conventional reform

(50CAN, Students First and others). The Alliance works hard to build influence with the U.S. Department of Education.

Single-unit, freestanding schools—still the majority—are disparaged as "mom and pop" schools. Prospective donors are shown the 'no excuses' schools: elementary schools, students often in uniform, learning English and math. Donors are thrilled to see young children in schools that look and feel like real school, serious school. Hearts warm; checkbooks open.

Results have been remarkable. The intense focus on improving the performance of elementary students has attracted substantial resources to support the start-up and expansion of schools. As the chartered sector has grown in some of the nation's largest and most troubled cities, donors sense they are at last getting American public education right. The Alliance keeps track of the changing market share of the district and chartered sectors in the cities: Washington, DC; New Orleans; Philadelphia and others.[16]

The schism in chartering has generated new issues

The new leadership has grown the chartered sector. In the process it has generated new controversy—with others, about the sector, and within the sector itself.

- Some of that controversy has to do with the prominence of "the heavy hitters". It was one thing when the sector consisted of small, free-standing schools started and operated by local people. It is something else for it to be so identified with large, even national, organizations backed by big foundations.

- There is debate within chartering about its relationship to the district sector. Is the goal to have the new models and new approaches that appear in chartered schools adopted by district

---

16. *See* the 2013 "Market Share" report on www.publiccharters.org.

schools? Or is the goal for the chartered sector to make itself so far as possible different from, better than, the district sector?[17]

- The implications of chartering for the district sector were not seen as, and realistically were not, a serious threat when the new sector was small. The perception changed when the sector came to have a large market share in some cities. It has strengthened with the sense there is now an intent for chartering to replace the district sector. In *The Futures of School Reform*, the 2012 report from the project organized by the Harvard Graduate School of Education, Jal Mehta identifies replacement as one of the possible scenarios. There is now in some quarters talk of a "post-district future".

- There is indecision, and controversy, within chartering about the idea of a single statewide authorizer. To some, this is the way to move the program most aggressively; the easiest way to shut down 'failing schools'. Others worry that, were the politics to turn against chartering, everything would stall; so prefer multiple authorlzers to hedge the bet.

- A major issue arises out of the Alliance's determination to recognize no concept of school performance except 'achievement' as measured by the state assessments. In June 2015 it got most of the state charter organizations to sign a statement affirming their commitment to 'quality' schools; 'quality defined implicitly as high scores on the tests. The next step, apparently, is to produce a national ranking of chartered schools, set against the ranking of district schools; using test-results at 4th, 8th and 10th grades, and graduation rates. Other concepts of performance, of quality, of success with students, are not recognized. People do read rankings; presumably this

---

17. Early, when chartering was seen as an R&D effort, it was assumed there would be a 'ripple effect', like a pebble dropped in a pond, its effects spreading. Quickly it became apparent that whether a new development in a chartered school has an effect on the district depends on the district. If the pond is frozen, the pebble dropped creates no ripple.

will validate chartering. Still: Why not let the chartered sector show its full range of successes?

- Another issue remaining, of course, has to do with the purpose of chartering; whether the early effort at innovation should be set aside and the goal narrowed to accountability. To some, the Alliance's almost Puritan orthodoxy carries a notion of achievement that is not in the interest of students and not in the interest of chartering itself. More will be said about this in Chapter 7.

All this has significantly changed the nature—and the perception—of chartering; has changed the debate about the chartered sector.

So, what to make of chartering today?

Itself an institutional innovation, the chartered sector looks much like most innovations in their early years, with people trying many variations of the new idea; displaying a mixture of successes and failures.

After the 'horseless carriage' appeared there were electric autos, steam-powered autos and gasoline-powered autos; there was front-wheel drive and rear-wheel drive; shaft drive and chain drive. It took time for the industry and the public to settle on the gasoline-powered, front-mounted engine with shaft drive to the rear wheels. (Now, in this self-improving system, innovation is appearing again.) It took time, as well, for the many companies that started building autos to consolidate into the industry we came to know.

After the Wright brothers flew successfully there were biplanes and monoplanes; planes with propellers pulling from the front and planes with propellers pushing from the rear. There was the unlamented auto-gyro and after that the helicopter. There were many manufacturers and many airlines. It took time for the airplane to evolve and for the aviation industry to consolidate.

You can easily think of other cases.

Today, in the wake of the states introducing chartering, we have much the same picture in public education—made more complex by the arrival of the digital electronics.

- The laws vary. Some states cap the size of the sector; some do not. In some states only the state may authorize schools; in others only the districts; in others a variety of entities may. Some states let commercial firms run schools; others do not. There are free-standing schools and there are 'charter management organizations'.

- Some schools are traditional in their approach to learning; others have moved to personalized, project-based, or blended learning. In a few schools the teachers are unionized; in most, not. Some schools are now organized with the teachers in charge, on the model of professional partnerships in law or medicine.

- There are successful schools and unsuccessful schools. There are quality operators and there are unscrupulous operators. There are success stories and there are scandals.

In time things will shake out. Successful designs, successful schools, will grow; unsuccessful schools will disappear and rip-off operators will be removed. You can see this process under way.

Inevitably, there is some impulse to 'take control' of the sector; to shape it and manage it; to control it. Some want to shut down its innovation.

Hopefully it will be left an 'open' sector, state policy leadership understanding how important the sector's evolution is to the success of public education; understanding, too, what serious problems would recur were the new sector to disappear.

Chartering remains critically important for improving K-12

Despite efforts to clarify, the confusion about chartering continues. That confusion is a problem. It makes state policy leadership uncertain which way to move.

The key for the states is to see their own interest clearly. No way would sensible legislators and governors find it helpful now to restore the 'exclusive franchise' and return to the public-utility model with which they struggled before they introduced chartering in the 1990s.

This means it is important not to debate the success of the new strategy only in terms of the schools currently produced. It is essential to keep in mind the rationale for opening K-12 to innovation, because innovation is the key to fundamental change.

To reestablish a serious effort at innovation the states might usefully do two things.

- **They might revisit chartering**, scraping off the regulatory barnacles so this sector can be the R&D sector it was intended to be. In the process they might make a serious effort to understand what kinds of schools, what innovations, are appearing.

- **They might look for ways other than chartering** to introduce innovation into their district sector. Part Three—Implementing—will come back to this critical question.

With the 'split screen' concept hopefully now clear, let's turn to the question how that strategy can make available to schools and teachers the opportunity to try the new-and-different, and consider what they might do with this opportunity.

PART TWO

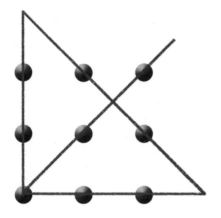

INNOVATING

CHAPTER 4

Innovation Is Schools and Teachers
Trying Things

Turn the conversation to 'innovation' and you are likely to hear people ask, "*What is* your innovation?"

That tells you right away that some effort to define innovation and to clarify the process of change is in order.

Innovation, invention, improvement, replication

Like most terms that have become excessively popular, 'innovation' has come to have multiple meanings. In a way the term spans three concepts, which need to be defined separately. These are:

- **Invention** . . . which John Lienhard defines as something new anywhere—though it can be considered an invention, he says, when a known thing is put to a new use. The steam engine, for example, was initially used to pump water out of coal mines; putting it to work later to pull a train and to drive a boat produced two important inventions in transportation.

- **Improvement** . . . which modifies an existing product or business model so it will work better. Things newly invented are almost always imperfect; need improvement: Think about 'the first' anything. In 1903 the Wright brothers, having seen the key was to be able to 'warp' the wings, essentially invented the airplane; made the first successful powered flight. Their airplane had two wings and had the elevators—the surfaces that control pitch, up or down—out in front. Think how rapidly improvements followed. In 1909 Bleriot built a single-wing aircraft and moved the elevators to the tail (where they have remained), then flew the English Channel. In 1927, after further improvements, Lindbergh flew the Atlantic in a plane like that.

- **Replication** . . . which is copying something earlier done elsewhere. Often much of what passes as 'innovation' is in truth replication; is simply new *here*. Replication sometimes involves improvements significant enough to qualify as innovation, as Bleriot's changes in aircraft design probably do. At the other extreme, the color telephone and the curly cord, which the Bell System thought of as innovations, probably do not.

Replication is a big industry in education. Research works to identify successful practices; an army of vendors and consultants works to spread these practices.

A key question is what to replicate. John Goodlad cautioned against the impulse, when some good school is discovered, to say: "Bottle it!" The impulse, that is, to replicate the school itself. Rather, he said, identify the conditions that permitted those schools to become good schools *and replicate those conditions.*[18]

That emphasis on 'the conditions' is reinforced by what Yale historian Paul Kennedy writes about the innovations critical to winning World War II. The story of those wartime innovations is fascinating in itself. More important is Kennedy's explanation of the role of innovation, and of what causes innovations to appear.[19]

---

18. See *Educational Renewal*, Chapter 7, "Tomorrow's Schools"; 1994.
19. See *Engineers of Victory: The Problem Solvers Who Turned the Tide in the Second World War*; 2013.

Create 'a climate of encouragement' for innovation

Setting goals and objectives, he writes, accomplishes nothing by itself. Objectives have to be realized. And that happens only when people find ways to solve the problems that stand in the way.

Because the education policy discussion is so largely a discussion about objectives . . . about what 'we must' do . . . I wrote commentaries for the *StarTribune* and for *Education Week* tying Kennedy's analysis of the wartime innovations to the situation in education.

To reach any goal, the key question is always: How?

'How?' was the question during World War II. Roosevelt and Churchill had their grand strategy—to supply Britain from factories in North America, to bomb Germany night and day, to open a second front in western Europe. But early 1943 was a dark time. Ships were being sunk, bombers shot down, at unsustainable rates. Winning would depend on figuring out how to get ships safely past the U-boats, how to provide fighter cover for the bombers over Germany, how to land an army on a hostile defended shore.

'How?' is the question, too, for education policy. It's fine to say we'll close achievement gaps, make graduates college-ready, enforce high standards, hold schools accountable and draw top candidates into teaching. But stating objectives does not make things happen. There has to be a How. And education policy is still searching for its How.

In *Engineers of Victory* Kennedy tells how the problems were solved in World War II:

- Canadian engineers replaced a bomb bay with an additional fuel tank, greatly extending the range of the B-24s patrolling the Atlantic for submarines.

- Physicists in Britain figured out how to miniaturize radar to fit in the nose cone of an airplane.

- Ronnie Harker, a Rolls-Royce test pilot, suggested putting the Spitfire's engine into the American P-51. That produced the Mustang—a fighter able to cover the B-17s all the way to Berlin and back.

- Unable after D-Day to get through the hedgerows, "a hillbilly from Tennessee" asked: Why not put some sharp teeth on the front of a tank; cut through those hedgerows? Sgt. Curtis Culin took the suggestion and welded blades onto the tanks, helping make the Normandy breakout possible.

- American Army engineers at Aberdeen Proving Ground turned the Soviet T-34 into a tank that drove the German panzers out of Russia.

So what was the How of the How?

It was, Kennedy says, leadership's "creation of a climate of encouragement for innovation". Solutions came not from the top but from those close to the action. "The successful systems," Kennedy writes, "stimulated initiative, innovation and ingenuity and encouraged problem solvers to tackle large, apparently intractable problems."

He concludes: "The winning of great wars requires people [to] run organizations . . . in a fashion that will allow outsiders to feed fresh ideas into the pursuit of victory. None of this can be done by the chiefs alone. There has to be a support system, a culture of encouragement, efficient feedback loops and a capacity to learn from setbacks."

The lesson, he believes, can be applied in other fields. America needs to apply it now to the struggle over education policy. This country has been fumbling around for almost 40 years, trying to find an effective strategy. In World War II, given the encouragement for innovation, the obstacles were cleared away in about 18 months.

Creating that 'climate of encouragement for innovation' is another example of the point Bill Andres was making . . . to think of change not as something you do but as something that happens when you do the fundamentals right. That was Goodlad's advice as well, about replicating *the conditions that caused the good schools to become good schools.*

Creating the conditions is 'getting the fundamentals right'.

Education policy needs to find an arrangement that will create that 'climate of encouragement'; that will replicate the conditions that permit and encourage people to make schools good schools.

Arguably, chartering fits this model: an R&D sector creating 'a condition' that encourages innovation. We will consider in Chapter 10 other ways state policy leadership can create the incentives—the reasons and opportunities—for people to try the new-and-different; to invent and to innovate.

The risk in trying things is not a serious objection

Always, somebody will worry about the risk associated with innovation. Critics of change, interests vested in the existing way of doing things, play on these fears: "What if . . . what if . . .?"

Innovation does involve risk, for students and for school. But a few things need to be said. Most important, that the risks in changing need to be set against the risk in *not* changing. We do need to worry about the downside of continuing with current strategy.

- There is risk in betting all the chips on assurances the nation's goals can be achieved with incremental improvement only; on assurances that 'accountability' will ensure student learning. Decades of disappointing results suggest this bet might lose.

- The traditional system and the traditional practices of schooling put many students at risk today. This—visible— failure is too easily tolerated. And the risk is not only for the students. Taxpayers are at risk as they trade money for promises. Elected officials go at risk for promises on which they cannot deliver. With K–12 not a conspicuously successful system, America is still 'a nation at risk'.

- There can be important rewards for innovation. These should not be put at risk.

A reasonable solution might be to adopt the concept of account-ability the country uses with its media. That is: no prior restraint. News-papers, magazines and the electronic media are not told in advance what they may and may not say . . . but can be held to account in the legal system or in the court of public opinion for injury their action imposes on others.

Innovation is 'not having to ask permission'

Doing-different *is* an unnatural act. Anything radical steps out into the unknown. That is bound to make people nervous. Someone will probably say the innovators should get permission to try such a thing.

Beware that idea. It will kill innovation.

A 'permission' system makes those giving permission responsible for what happens. They will then want to limit *their* risk. They will ask the innovators for assurance the new/different will succeed; something the innovators of course cannot provide.

Finding success not assured, those in authority are likely to reject the proposal. Or to limit their approval to something they feel is 'safe'. Worse: Forcing schools and teachers to get permission, asking them to guarantee success, will keep them from proposing any truly significant change.

Net: A 'get-permission' approach will kill innovation; will reduce it to replication. Resist that pressure.

Let the risks lie with the innovators. Happily, there are common-sense ways for teachers, schools and districts to minimize the risks.

- Keep the scale of the changes small. The errors will then be small and can be quickly and easily corrected.

- Keep participation voluntary. Innovation needs to be, and almost always is, arranged to be a choice for families, for teachers and for districts. Without choice, innovation is blocked.

- Be sensible about accountability. If something has clearly proved a bad idea, stop doing it. Some entity should have the authority to intervene where necessary. On the other hand: Accept that there will be some failure and that this is OK.

The other key rule is: Don't give up. Don't expect the innovation to work perfectly in its initial form. Nothing does: Think about 'the first' anything. The course of innovation never runs smooth. There will be moments when the 'new' seems like a success; there will be moments when people are almost ready to give up. Keep going; keep trying variations on the original idea. Some years back an article in the Economist carried a graphic nicely illustrating 'the ups and downs' of innovation. It's below; used with permission.

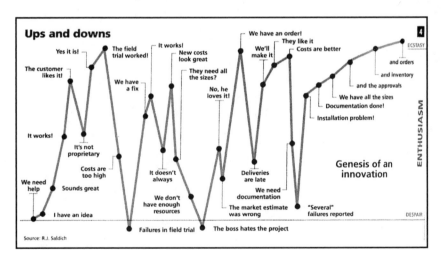

It will be important also to find a way to protect the small green shoots of innovation against the opposition—always claiming to protect the public interest—that comes from groups concerned their private interests might be affected adversely were the innovations to succeed.

Successful innovations should not be shut down because their disruptive effect upsets other parties. Some way should be arranged for there to be an entity to which a school could appeal when attacked in this way.

Remember (to say it yet again): The innovation side of the 'split screen' does not have to be large. Just big enough for some reasonable number of schools to be created in a sector where 'the 'conditions' are right for people to try things.

Let's consider now what those innovations might involve.

CHAPTER 5

Above All, Try Personalizing Learning To Maximize Student Motivation

When president of Public Agenda, Deborah Wadsworth would sometimes quote Daniel Yankelovich on the importance of 'discretionary effort'.

His concept was that in any organization there is a level of effort all employees will give you—to keep their jobs, if nothing else. There is a higher level of effort they will give you if motivated to do so. Your job in running organizations—probably also in designing organizations—is to elicit that extra level of discretionary effort.

In education people usually think of the teacher as the worker. But clearly students are co-workers on the job of learning. Student effort matters, for achievement. So it would seem important to find ways to elicit from students that extra level of discretionary effort.

Frymier: To motivate, know the differences among students

In a long afternoon discussion with Education|Evolving in 1999 Jack Frymier laid out the case for making motivation central, and talked about how to do that. Frymier spent his career on the curriculum and instruction side of public education: first as a teacher and administrator and then as a professor at Ohio State University before moving to Phi Delta Kappa.

Here's what he said.

- Students learn when they're motivated to learn. If they want to learn, they will; if they don't, you probably can't make 'em. *Any successful effort to improve learning will therefore be fundamentally about improving students' motivation.*

- Motivation is individual. Young people differ in personality, in background and experience, in sociability, in creativity, in intelligence, in their interests and aptitudes. Different students are motivated by different things. No effort at motivation will succeed unless it works with these differences.

- 'School' is not very well tuned to the differences among students. Teachers might know students less well today than in the past. Schools are pressed now to be interested mainly in what students know and can do, less in who they are. Students move around, are moved around. Schools are age-graded: Students are with a teacher for a year; next year, have another. Schools are larger: As Ted Sizer has pointed out, high school teachers especially have far too many students to know any of them well.

- Curriculum materials are not often adapted to individual students.

- Teaching methods are not often varied according to the needs and interests of the individual student. Some teachers do this, but many do not. Teachers work mostly with students in groups; most are obsessed with 'classroom management'. Most teachers talk too much (as Professor John Goodlad also reported from his research in *A Place Called School*).

- Adapting materials and methods to individual student needs is a teachable skill. It just isn't very often taught where teachers are trained.

- Teachers aren't given much opportunity to modify 'instruction' in this way. The curriculum is 'sequenced'; teachers are not encouraged to modify the order in which things are taught or the amount of time that is spent on what. Students are not free to pursue a topic that interests them: The schedule calls for the course to move on.

- There are no rewards and few opportunities for teachers trying to modify teaching in this way, so that learning becomes interesting to the student and becomes the responsibility of the student.

- Because school takes this form, most academic subjects are not of interest to most students. If it weren't for the extracurriculars there would be a revolution by young people in school.

Whole-class instruction means the teacher is confronted with a room full of students having a wide range of interests, aptitudes, attainment-levels, motivations. As Albert Shanker pointed out on the anniversary of the new Saturn school in Saint Paul, that creates a dilemma for the teacher. Teaching to the middle might seem the obvious answer, but that bores the students who learn quickly and leaves behind the students who learn more slowly.

Personalization, Shanker said, is the way out.

There must be a way for schools and teachers to adapt the learning program to the differences they find among their students.

What to do to maximize motivation

As Frymier said: It is hard to see school today as organized with student interest and effort primarily in mind. Ask in a meeting some-time who would rise to defend the proposition that conventional school is arranged to maximize student motivation: See how many stand.

• •

I once put Frymier's proposition—that any successful effort to improve learning will begin by improving student motivation—to a key person in the 'standards' movement.

"I don't buy that", he said.

"Well", I asked, "how will you get students to make the effort needed to meet high standards?"

He said, "There are a lot of people working very hard on that".

I persisted: "Who, for example?"

"Try Jim McPartland at Johns Hopkins", he said.

A few days later I called McPartland; put the question to him.

"Well", he said, "you have to start with motivation."

• •

Two objections lie in the way of what Frymier proposed.

One is that personalization is a bad idea. There really are people influential in the policy discussion who feel that to begin with what interests students is to start down a 'slippery slope' that leads to the dreaded 'constructivism'; who believe that it is, rather, for adults to decide what students should learn.

The other and more important objection is that personalization is just not possible. People see teachers having all they can do to manage and instruct the 25 students as a class. "Now you're telling me they are supposed to work with each of the 25 individually? I don't get that."

That was in fact the reaction at the conference on innovation that Jobs for the Future sponsored in Boston in 2009. Immediately it was clear that to visualize personalized learning you have to stop seeing the traditional classroom. Richard Kazis put into the final report the photo that appears in this book, on the first page of the color insert, showing students at their work-stations studying independently.[20] That photo has gone all around the country.

---

20. To see that school, go to www.mncs.k12.mn.us.

The project-based learning in that school fits Frymier's prescription. Its 'advisers' start by asking each student 'What are you most interested in; most curious about?' and build a learning program around the answer.

In that school a staff person from the Education Commission of the States found a boy interested in why people were getting elected to and unelected from the state board of education in Kansas based on their position about evolution. A teacher could build on that: understand something about genetics, read Darwin, study the impact of his work on religion in 19th-century Britain, read *Inherit the Wind* about the Scopes trial in Tennessee . . . pretty soon you have a project that pulls together history, geography, zoology, theology and political science.

. . . .

A fascinating case of a teacher personalizing learning in his third-grade classroom—'trying something'—appeared in Minnesota in a district near Saint Paul about 2008.

He had grown up in south India; came to America to study graphics. Halfway through a career in the printing industry he decided to become a teacher. On the job he soon found that what he had been trained to do and told to do was not effective.

The September assessments showed the level of attainment among his students ranging from the 10th percentile and below to the 90th percentile and above. He concluded he had to individualize.

He asked if he could cash out the value of the whiteboard the district proposed to give him. The administrators said no. So he used his own and his wife's money and some contributed dollars to buy PCs, software, voice recorders and printed materials. He selected gaming software for the students to learn English and math.

His classroom has been transformed. Students are active, moving, talking to each other; totally engaged. He changed the technology from whole-class instruction to personalized learning.[21]

Clearly this is not replicable. This teacher came from a non-traditional background. He acted on his own. He was willing himself to finance the new technology of personalized learning. (See Chapter 8.) The district at the time was not supportive; did not appreciate his setting-aside its regular curriculum materials.

---

21. To see this story go to http://www.educationevolving.org/pai

But his effort carries some important lessons about the potential for teacher-initiative, to which we will return in Chapter 11, and about the system-difficulty with change. Note in the video the teacher's comment about the response when he presented his results; the "bureaucratic apathy" he encountered.

· ·

Electronics by themselves do not personalize learning: It is possible to put the classroom textbook on-screen. A wonderful photo taken from the rear of a classroom shows a laptop open on every student desk—and the same picture on every screen. But electronics have the capacity to personalize learning, helping students learn in and out of school.

Clearly personalization does change the nature of teachers' work. And surely the teachers could use help in their new role.

Help for the teacher in personalizing learning can come from students helping other students. A superintendent in North St. Paul remembered how, when a teacher, he would use 'slower' students in the upper grades to tutor students in the lower grades. That worked for the younger students, and the experience of becoming a kind of teacher proved, he found, immensely reinforcing for those older students.

Digital electronics—again, look at the photo—almost certainly will be critical in personalizing learning. Equally, the effort at personalization—project-based learning or an effort to break with age-grading—might help realize the potential of digital electronics.[22]

Personalization opens the door to competency-based learning. This is tricky, though. It is one thing for a school to give credit for knowledge and skills a student acquires, wherever s/he gets them. It is something else, a bigger challenge, for a school to let students move ahead as fast as their competencies accumulate. Advocates of 'blended learning' often suggest it implies competency-based in the latter sense, but concede in private that to date 'blended' remains captive to age-grading.

---

22. The New Schools Venture Fund 'summit' in 2009 featured an Oxford-style debate: 'Resolved: That computers will revolutionize learning'—or something like that. Larry Cuban, long a skeptic about the effect of computers in classrooms, was arguing the negative. Joanne Weiss, moderating, gave the final question to a person in the audience who said: "I wonder whether, if we pulled out the assumption of age-grading, Professor Cuban might move to the other side of the argument". And Larry said: "I would".

Why would we not start with what seems most obvious?

If motivation might in fact be the key to eliciting the discretionary effort so important for learning, there surely is reason to be concerned that motivation barely appears in the conventional strategy for improvement.

The key step is to encourage schools to move to some form of personalized learning. Students moving at their own pace would learn more: Those who need more time would get more time, and those who could go faster would go faster.

Motivation, eliciting that extra level of effort, seems important also for the economics of education. Anything extra we get from students comes for free: *Why would we not want to enlarge the role of the worker we do not pay?*

Letting students specialize, move as fast as they can demonstrate their competence, seems likely to motivate young people to learn. It certainly seems something to try on the innovation side of the 'split screen' . . . while the mainline system continues with whole-class instruction and age-based progression.

CHAPTER 6

Get Past the Old Institution of Adolescence

Speaking of motivation . . . why does the whole effort to improve learning go on with no one questioning the institution of adolescence that works so powerfully against it?

In years of listening to the education policy discussion I had never heard adolescence mentioned as a problem until Shelton White, then professor of psychology at Harvard, put it in perspective at the gathering held for Ted Sizer when he left Brown University in May 1999.

"A separate society for the young, prolonging childhood" was how White described it; created a century ago by a coming-together of the child welfare movement, the laws against child labor, the new high schools and the special legislation for juvenile offenders.

Whose interest does 'adolescence' serve?

Earlier in America, and in many parts of the world still, you were adult at puberty. Up to 1905, about 40 percent of American 16-year-olds were in school and about 40 percent in work. Some of that work was exploitive and dangerous, in mines and factories. Soon that began to change, young people moving rapidly out of work.

To absorb those millions of teenagers America vastly expanded high school. Today about 90 percent of 16-year-olds are in school. And a popular notion now is to keep students in school even longer.

Like most reforms, this one was filled with good intentions. But its effect has been to discriminate against those young people whose experience, aptitudes or inclination does not fit them for academic work. It blocks those whose abilities and experiences enable them to achieve more, sooner. And it removes work as an important dimension of learning.

Those creating the institution of adolescence were not moved solely by a concern for child welfare. Organized labor, then growing in influence, wanted young people out of the labor force. And as White noted, adolescence created millions of jobs for adult professionals: people in corrections, in social work—and in schools. The institution of education is vested, deeply complicit, in the institution of adolescence.

"Adults have disappeared from the lives of adolescents," Deborah Meier, founder of the Central Park East School in New York City, said that day at Brown. "We have deliberately created [schools] in which it is impossible for adults to know kids well. Young people know no one but their peers. And all this gets worse the closer they get to adulthood."

Young people still do work, as someone pointed out at the Sizer gathering. But not so they can advance: They work so they can earn money for college and so they can be marketed to as consumers.

A century after it appeared, the institution of adolescence is itself a given. Most everyone today accepts the assertion that school is the route upward. Earlier, work was. But increasingly the world of work is closed until one has the credentials provided by school. The idea seems to be that young people will get in school everything they need to prepare them for life and career. In school today vocational training has been eclipsed by academic study.

Does this make sense? Think about the people you know . . . read the obituaries of people . . . who got lots of life-experiences early, out of school and at work.[23]

When young people get responsibility early, what do they do?

Some years after the discussion at Brown I came across an *Education Week* commentary titled "Let's Abolish High School". It was written

---

23. We will return to this question of success and achievement in Chapter 7.

by Robert Epstein, a student of White's and by then a professor at the University of California at San Diego.

Epstein quickly disclaimed a serious intention to do away with high school. He was trying, he wrote, to get people to think about the damage the institution of adolescence does to young people and to our society. He is serious about that, as he explains fully in *The Case Against Adolescence* (now retitled *Teen 2.0*).

Epstein does not disagree about the moronic behavior of many teens. But he says adolescence 'infantilizes' young people. Deny them serious responsibilities, keep them out of real work, give them virtually no contact with adults, tell them they have no function except to be schooled (and marketed to): Why wouldn't they behave as they do?

I drew on his analysis in 2008 when *Education Next* asked me to review *The Dumbest Generation* by Mark Bauerlein, a professor of English at Emory University. The book is an assault on people under 30, obsessed with their digital devices, disinclined to read and almost unable to write.

I quoted what Paul Johnson, a British popular historian, wrote in *The Birth of the Modern* about the accomplishments in the years after 1815 by young people who came from truly disadvantaged backgrounds, who had almost no schooling and who went to work early.

It was a time when new fields of activity provided opportunities for young people to get serious responsibilities early and to rise as rapidly as their abilities and energies would take them. They did amazing things. Some of their roads, bridges and other public works still stand in England, still in use.

- Michael Faraday, the scientist, "was born poor, the son of a Yorkshire blacksmith. He had no education other than a few years at a school for the poor, but as a bookbinder's apprentice he read the works he bound . . ."

- John Otley, the geologist, "had no education apart from village schooling and set up as a basket-maker."

- James Naysmith, the engineer, "started as an apprentice coach painter. His son, James, inventor of the steam hammer, made a brass cannon at the age of nine."

- Henry Maudsley, "perhaps the greatest of all the machine-tool inventors, began work at 12 as a powder-monkey in a cartridge works."

- Matthew Murray, "the great engine designer, began as a kitchen boy and butler. Richard Roberts, brilliant inventor of power looms, was a shoemaker's son, had virtually no education and began as a quarry laborer. John Kennedy, the first great builder of iron ships, was another poor Scot who received no schooling except in summer and started as a carpenter's boy."

In *Longitude*, Dava Sobel tells the story of John Harrison, who solved "the greatest scientific problem of his time". With no formal education and no apprenticeship to any watchmaker, he invented a clock that would carry the true time from the home port to any point in the world, enabling mariners at last to know their east/west location.

In *The Maritime History of Massachusetts*, Samuel Eliot Morison writes about Mary Patten, wife of the captain of a clipper ship. "In 1858 on a voyage around Cape Horn, her husband fell ill. The first mate was in irons for insubordination; the second mate was ignorant of navigation. Mrs. Patten had made herself mistress of the art of navigation during a previous voyage. She took command, and for 52 days she navigated the ship of 1800 tons, tending her husband the while, and took both safely into San Francisco". She was 19.

Wartime generates many such stories. In *With Wings Like Eagles: A History of the Battle of Britain*, Michael Korda writes that by late-summer 1940 more and more of those flying the Spitfires and Hurricanes were—in our terms—high school seniors. Nineteen-year-old women were ferrying the planes from the factories to the aerodromes. In Russia, Nadia Popova started flying at 16, and at 18 flew hundreds of missions in flimsy plywood aircraft, bombing German encampments at night. At

18 Cecil Phillips in America and Mavis Lever in England had begun breaking codes.

I ended the review by asking:

> Are we to believe that these abilities have been lost, in young people today? Or is our society simply failing to let young people have, early, the responsibilities and opportunities needed for them to achieve?

What 'adolescence' costs young people—and costs society

Adolescence simultaneously relieved young people of responsibilities and brought prohibitions that denied them opportunities. If you're not an adult you may not do adult things: be employed full-time, inherit property, vote, seek or refuse medical treatment, sign contracts, file lawsuits, marry without parental consent. One insurance company still pushes to raise the legal driving age to 18.

After 1950, the effects were compounded by the cultural shift that public-opinion analyst Daniel Yankelovich details in *New Rules*—from the ethic of self-denial to the ethic of self-fulfillment. So many people had so much money that it was impossible to say no to cars, clothes, guitars, computers, travel. No wonder youth behavior changed dramatically. With prosperity, a new youth culture appeared: music, dress, drugs, sex.

Adults, disliking this teenage behavior, tried to control it, tightening the restrictions. Which of course bred resentment, stimulating still more challenging behavior. Which generated still more restrictions. Curfews. Can't drive. Can't drink. "No entry except with adult". Blocked access to the Internet. Sex under 18 criminalized. No cigarettes. Dress codes. "Parental Consent Required". And in school, metal detectors, video surveillance, armed guards, no hoods and "No cellphones!"

The restrictions built into the institution of adolescence have made young people arguably the most-discriminated-against class of people in our society. And nobody sees it. Good people who would never utter a racial or ethnic slur think nothing of referring to young adults as 'kids'.

Though told education is the only way up, most young people find the schooling they are offered neither motivating nor relevant, affording them little say in what they study, in how and how rapidly they learn or in the way their school runs.

Few things about the education policy discussion are more stunning than the absence of the student voice. You go to meeting after meeting and seldom if ever hear a student consulted. It is almost entirely an adult discussion. Why, for heaven's sake? Who knows more about school and learning? How many organizations would not care to learn what the users think of their service?

Perhaps adults in the K–12 system fear what students might say. When Elinor Burkett was looking to spend a year in a suburban high school, after Columbine, principals told her in effect: "You have to be crazy to think I'd let you see what goes on in my school". Read *Another Planet*: Think how different it is from the picture of high school the public is shown in the education policy literature and in the media; the happy group of well-dressed students.

But—uncomfortable as it might prove—why *not* seek the advice of those who know most about what goes on in school? Most important: What if those talents *are* still there in young people, suppressed by the institution of adolescence?

This country could be getting far more from its young people

It will take years to dismantle the institution of 'adolescence'—as it has taken years to dismantle other obsolete social institutions. The way to begin, though, is to create some schools that let young people demonstrate their maturity; learn as much and as rapidly as possible and go as far in every field as their efforts and abilities will take them.

Schools in the innovation sector of the 'split screen' strategy would introduce competency-based progression—as per Chapter 5. They would move more young people into essentially adult roles earlier in life, as John Goodlad and others proposed. They could open new opportunities for work, crediting and respecting, as employers often do, what young people learn outside school.

Here are two examples from just one community college near where I live.

- In 2009, while finishing eighth grade (at 13), Caleb Kumar earned an associate of arts degree from North Hennepin Community College. At 15, he received a $25,000 scholarship from the Davidson Institute for Talent Development for developing an algorithm to automate the diagnosis of bladder cancer.

- In 1998, Rob and Ryan Weber, twins, got AA degrees from North Hennepin through Minnesota's post-secondary enrollment option just before graduating from Osseo Senior High. They'd already been starting computer software businesses. Today, NativeX, a firm they started in 2000 with older brother Aaron, has over 160 employees and offices in Sartell (Minnesota), Minneapolis and San Francisco.

You might have seen the film about Laura Dekker. She was single-handling boats in Holland at six. At 13 she decided she wanted to sail alone around the world. The authorities had a fit—mostly about her leaving school—but her parents agreed. At 14 she set off in a 38-foot ketch, stopped along the way, returned safely at 16.

America could get far more from its young people if it did adapt school to let them move faster. Google for 'youth accomplishment': You'll see that outside school young people today are doing things we usually associate with adults. But this is mostly in fields adults can't master or don't want to enter: sports, entertainment, digital electronics. The routines of school, the institution of adolescence, block off young people from opportunities to do more sooner in mainline fields.

Accelerating learning, moving students on to post-secondary at 16, is positive for the economics of education as well. Minnesota, for example, has about 75,000 juniors and 75,000 seniors, spends about $10,000 on each. Multiply $10,000 by 150,000, and you get a rather large number. And that's *per year*. And Minnesota is less than 2 percent of the nation.

How might we release this reservoir of talent?

An effort in either sector to innovate with school would not directly reach the institution of adolescence which lies outside it, surrounds it and influences it. A real attack on this problem lies outside the area of education policy. But if someone, somewhere—in journalism, in politics, in a foundation—were to make this a cause, were to suggest that young people are a major untapped reservoir of talent in our economy . . . things might change for the better in schools.

We could start by picking up Epstein's idea to make adultness competency-based rather than age-based. He does not suggest abolishing 'adolescence'. He proposes that young people be allowed to test out of its restrictions—as he says many could. He has developed an assessment of 'adultness'—of responsibility and maturity—given thousands of times. Between the ages of 15 and 85, Epstein finds, the proportion of persons demonstrating those qualities is essentially independent of age.

Some schools we see in the chartered sector do treat young people more as adults. Avalon School in Saint Paul, for example, has a constitution that delegates to students significant authority over dress and conduct. The school finds the students make and enforce stricter rules than its adults could make and enforce.

The reluctance of mainline school to move with this idea argues for involving the organizations that work with youth outside of school.

We could enlarge the role of the non-school learning organizations: the science museums and art galleries and zoos and organizations such as 4-H. These are cautious about suggesting they 'educate' young people: They worry that the K–12 institution, better financed and possessive about its claim on learning, would block them out or try to take them over. But there is potential here.

Trusting teens, treating them more like adults, is an idea unlikely to be adopted quickly. But it would be worth trying: People often do live up to what's expected of them.

CHAPTER 7

Broaden the Concept of 'Achievement'

Judging by the discussion about achievement you might think its definition is not in dispute. Surely it is how well students and schools score on the state assessments: What else?

With that clear, why would there be any need to innovate with the concept of achievement?

Actually, some further thinking would be a good idea. 'The box' drawn around the definition of achievement by the education policy discussion is remarkably tight; fails to include many dimensions of achievement that are real and that are important to the learning of young people.

It will be good to question the conventional wisdom about achievement. But it will not be easy to get people thinking beyond the conventional definition: that achievement means learning to read and write English and to do mathematics. Scoring well on the assessments is the measure of that achievement. If students score well, your school has achieved.

Surely proficiency in English and math is the foundation for other learning, later. But that narrow definition leaves a lot left to be done. This country is not going to make it on proficiency alone. A concept of achievement narrowed that far omits too much. There are dimensions of academics beyond English and math; there are dimensions of achievement beyond academics. And there is a need for achievement beyond elementary school.

We need a better definition of 'achievement'

Look at the graphic below. The inner hemisphere captures the areas on which the discussion currently focuses: elementary students as the 'who', basic skills and proficiency as the 'what', and the technology of whole-class instruction as the 'how'.

Now look at the outer hemisphere. Are we not concerned with the achievement of high school students? Or about knowledge beyond the academic? What about the personal dimension of achievement, the "every student will learn" that every district insists is its mission?

Field of Achievement

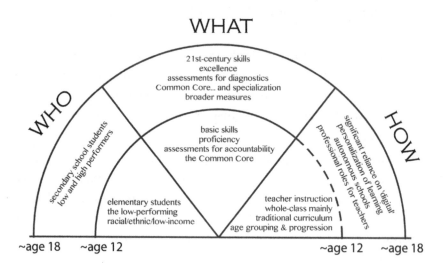

The discussion about achievement (and its measurement) in this country is a low-grade discussion. It needs to be better. It can be better.

The conventional definition misses some real achievement

There is a special problem in identifying the achievement of nontra-ditional students. A broader definition might show that those put down as 'low achieving' might have skills and knowledge simply not covered by the current definition, and so not picked up by current assessments.

Bob Wedl, Minnesota's former commissioner of education, suggests the narrow current view diminishes the achievement of racial and ethnic minorities. If we were to define achievement as the ability to speak two or more languages, he asks, which students would be 'high-achieving'?[24]

Student scores are not a measure of school quality

Just as high scores alone do not fully define achievement for a student, high scores do not establish success for a school. It is important to listen to the statisticians. They are firm that it is statistically invalid and intellectually indefensible to use student mean proficiency scores on standardized tests as the measure of *school* quality.[25]

'Quality' is never one-dimensional, is it?

The question of defining quality in a school does go to basic concepts of what matters. Ask people you know to name an area of life in which the concept of quality is one-dimensional. See how many will.

In most areas of life 'quality' is multidimensional. Most anything you can name has some dimensions you value highly and some you do not. Think about your car. There is initial cost and operating cost, there is miles-per-gallon and frequency-of-repair; there is capacity and speed; there is safety, style and color. It's the same with your house, your neighborhood, your city, your job, the organization you work for. Probably also with people you know. Evaluations are multidimensional and judgments about quality are made on balance. True?

So, can we apply to schools this sensible approach we use in other areas of life? Might not a multi-dimensional definition of quality and

---

24. A middle-school principal told Wedl about a recent East African immigrant child who on a visit to the Minneapolis Institute of Arts ran excitedly to one of the exhibits and read his classmates what was written there. It was written, of course, in Arabic.

25. See, for example, the Angoff lecture given for ETS in 2004 by Professor Stephen Raudenbush, now at the University of Chicago. Or read and come to grips with what John Tanner writes in *The Pitfalls of Reform: Its Incompatibility with Actual Improvement*; 2014.

of achievement be appropriate? More important: Might a multidimensional definition be fairer both to students and to schools, in establishing failure? Jack Frymier thought it terribly wrong for adults not themselves at risk to be imposing failure on young people just getting started in life.

Achievement is also what you can do with what you know

Until recently, achievement was pretty much about what the student knew. Now, increasingly the question is: What can you do with what you know?

Ted Sizer argued the object is to get young people to "use their minds well"—perhaps echoing Whitehead, who counseled in *The Aims of Education* against "inert ideas": Education, he wrote, "is the acquisition of the art of the utilisation of knowledge".

The Programme for International Student Achievement (PISA) tests the ability to apply knowledge—which is perhaps why students in America do not score well on this international assessment.

Hewlett Foundation and others are raising the importance of "deeper learning". The Bill & Melinda Gates Foundation is talking about "next-generation learning". If you have heard David Coleman talk about his concept of the Common Core you know he is insistent on students being able to understand and to explain serious material they have read.

The question 'what can you do?' also looks beyond school toward what young people will, practically, be able to do and be able to earn, in life. That suggests attention to vocational skills—which challenges the preference among educators for moving young people into academic work; challenges the notion that school rather than work is the way to advance in the modern economy. It challenges parents' desire for their offspring 'to go to college'; challenges the bias against careers in which their children "get their hands dirty".

CHAPTER 7

Some achievement lies in 'noncognitive' knowledge and skills

There is a growing conviction that non-academic skills also matter: critical thinking ... creativity ... the ability to communicate well ... the ability to collaborate and to work well with others. These appear to be important not only in themselves but also because they assist in developing academic knowledge and skills. The Partnership for 21st Century Skills now offices with the Council of Chief State School Officers.

Professor James Heckman at the University of Chicago has written and spoken extensively about this. Paul Tough's *How Children Succeed* relies heavily on Heckman's work; cites "persistence, self-control, curiosity, conscientiousness, grit and self-confidence" as important.

Traditionalists resist—disparaging nonacademic skills as 'soft'; arguing that these can't be defined and can't be measured so needn't be considered. But what if these skills are important? And what if they *can* be measured?

On the question of what's achievement, business appears confused. As Joe Graba has pointed out, chief executives and public-affairs officers have tended to come into the policy discussion behind the effort to improve academic skills, strongly supporting standards. Closer to the point of hire, and among those in human resources, people in business are less interested in the school transcript and in the scores.

Listen to Lowell Hellervik, whose firm of 'selection psychologists', Personnel Decisions, Inc., created a test now given millions of times in a variety of industries and organizations for a variety of jobs:

> Clearly, cognitive skills are important for success both in schools and outside school. However, anyone who claims that cognitive clout is the only thing that matters flies in the face of hiring authorities' personal experience as well as the scientific data. . . . Employers and many academics who studied the test found it to be a significant predictor of success for people in many jobs, a predictor of "conscientiousness". Conscientiousness is highly prized by organizations; is a personal characteristic that does not require traditional cognitive skills. It can

be taught, since its components are behavioral, such as getting to work on time.

For a school, achievement might lie in 'beating the odds'

Schools whose scores are not near the top in the state or in the district might still be high-achieving schools. Schools that enroll students who are 16 years old and reading at fourth-grade level cannot properly be faulted for not graduating those students at age 17. These still might be good schools; quality schools; high-achieving schools with their students learning more every year.

Some in schools with over-age/under-credited students, or with a high proportion of students in some way educationally disadvantaged, often say they are 'beating the odds'. That is a real, a valid, concept. It does require definition. The object is to identify the value added by a teacher and/or school during the course of the year and over time.

Here is a definition, worked out with a professional in research and evaluation in a big-city district:

> 'Beating the odds', as a measure of achievement, is about identifying the progress a particular student has made in a given year and relating that to the progress this student would statistically be expected to have made given the student's prior achievement and demographic background (special education status, home language, family income, race, gender and English Language Learner status).

The progress identified for a particular student can then be compared with (a) the progress made by other students with the same prior achievement and demographic background and (b) the progress made by that student and by other students in other years.

The measures of individual students' progress can be aggregated to show the progress made by a given teacher's class or by a given school; indicating whether or not the class or school is 'beating the odds'. What emerges can be compared to the progress made by other classes and other schools with similar characteristics, to show which teachers and schools are doing relatively better at 'beating the odds'.

This more careful definition accepts the statisticians' insistence that high scores on tests do not by themselves demonstrate either 'success' for a student or 'performance' for a school. The scores might reflect the demographic makeup of that school.

Conversely, a student, class or school might be succeeding—beating the odds'; making greater progress than would be expected—even though scores, "the level of performance", are low. 'Beating the odds' is not defined simply by relating scores to the proportion of students on 'free and reduced lunch': That is only one part of the background to be considered in assessing 'the odds' of a student, class or school making more than a year's progress in a year's time.

Assessment, too, should be multi-dimensional

The tests of achievement should ask young people to show what they can do as well as what they know.

It is interesting to talk with people in the building trades about the kind of programs they operate as they prepare young people to be, say, an electrician; low-voltage or high-voltage. There is classroom learning. But learning the theory is not enough. The student must show a journeyman electrician s/he can do all the things an electrician will have to do on the job.[26]

Most of us have experience with this dual concept of achievement and assessment. It is what we find in driver education: having to learn the rules and also to show the highway patrol officer you can drive according to the rules.

Most important, perhaps: Individualize achievement

The policy discussion today seems overwhelmingly about aggregates. It looks at the achievement of schools, of racial groups, of states and nations. It looks at aggregates in fields and subjects of study; at how

---

26. Those running training programs in the trades like to point out also that in apprenticeship the student earns while learning. And, not incidentally, that the AGC scale for plumbers in the Twin Cities area is now about $80,000 a year.

many students fall into which category: below basic, basic, proficient, advanced.

Yet achievement starts with the individual student, does it not? And individual students differ. Interests differ. Motivation differs. If individuals differ in many respects then should our concept of a young person achieving also be individualized?

Even aptitudes differ. You do not hear much about aptitude differences in the education policy discussion. This is curious because aptitudes are real and are important for learning. Psychologists have found that different individuals really are good at different things. There is more than one way of being smart and more than one way of learning, as Howard Gardner demonstrated in his work on 'multiple intelligences'.

Work by the Ball Foundation with psychologists at the University of Minnesota led to the creation of the Ball Aptitude Battery. This assessment can distinguish aptitudes that are verbal, conceptual and abstract from those that are spatial, visual and tactile.[27]

A risk is that school people—whose aptitudes tend to be verbal, abstract and conceptual—sometimes define those aptitudes as 'smart'. So they regard students whose aptitudes are spatial, visual and tactile as 'not smart'. The risk is that they counsel these students into careers for which they are not suited and thus into lives that are frustrating and unsuccessful.

Bob Wedl argues that the standards for achievement should be individual. It is ridiculous, he suggests, to think that the math standard for students generally would be appropriate for a student looking to major in science or engineering. Conversely, a standard high enough for the student in engineering would probably be inappropriate for a student heading for a career in art.

A former governor recently spoke disapprovingly of "setting the bar at a different height for each student". Yet if excellence is the objective, then perhaps standards *should* be set relative to the individual student's goals and to the individual student's potential. A teenage boy should be

---

27. John Goodlad, speaking to the alumni of the University of Minnesota College of Education, told about his two sons. One, he said, could understand a clock if you explained how a clock worked. The other understood a clock only when he took it apart to see how it worked.

able to jump chest-height. But many can jump higher—try to, and do, in the competition of a track meet. The bar keeps being raised for the best.

It is important to be realistic. If we define successful performance as all students clearing the same height, and if the bar is set high, the failure rate for students and schools is likely to be high—which will not be tolerable politically. But set the bar low and the country will not get the learning it needs. Individualizing standards seems the logical answer.

Thinking in terms of individualizing achievement opens the discussion into the important question about 'excellence'. Excellence needs to be a goal, along with proficiency. And excellence usually involves specialization.

In high school students can specialize in athletics; cannot specialize nearly to the same degree in academics.

It is far from unusual to see seventh-graders playing varsity sports: in tennis, especially; also in hockey. Natalie Darwitz went up to the varsity hockey team when she was in seventh grade. Her school that year went to the state tournament. In that tournament she scored nine goals. She went on to star at the University of Minnesota and in the world championships. She has three Olympic medals.

She was not required at the same time to play volleyball and softball and to run track. She could specialize. Excellence *does* imply specialization.

Progression, then, might also be individualized

The question is hard to escape: Why not let high school students specialize also with academics? If indeed this country could be getting far more from its young people . . . eliciting that extra level of discretionary effort . . . something like specialization would seem to make sense.

Specialization implies competency-based progression.

Traditional school has made time the constant, learning the variable. Some students need more time; some finish the course in half the allotted time. There has long been a sense that time should be the variable. That is something to try in the innovation sector, in the 'split screen' strategy.

Competency-based progression challenges conventional school, in which age-grading has been a given. It is common to think in terms of 'grades'. People ask a child, "What grade are you in?" Educators ask, "Is this student at grade level?"

The current national effort to improve standards and assessment accepts age-grading. At the Atlanta meeting of the Education Commission of the States in 2012, Mike Cohen, head of Achieve, was asked why he had been discussing the Common Core entirely in terms of grade-levels. Mike said: "We take the system as it stands. It is an age-graded system."

But again, in the interest of maximizing excellence, why not encourage some schools to try breaking free of age-grading?

Assessment can be individualized, along with achievement

Schools in the innovation sector should perhaps individualize testing, too; particularly in the early years when testing should be diagnostic, used primarily to ensure all are on track to be proficient in reading at age eight.

That might distress those in conventional school reform who believe the purpose of testing is to generate aggregate data that can be used to separate 'good teachers' from 'bad teachers'. But perhaps the purpose of testing really should be diagnostic; to help students learn. Would it not be better to use testing positively to identify the students lagging in their learning, with whom teachers need to intervene?

Educators who use the approach (rather ungracefully) termed Response to Intervention (RtI) start where each child is; check continually to see whether each is on track to proficiency in reading by third grade; correct the instruction if a child is not.

They describe traditional whole-group instruction as "Wait, to Fail", allowing those students slow to learn to fall farther and farther behind until they are referred into special education. RtI, they suggest, might be termed 'Correct, to Succeed'. Disability, to put it plainly, might lie more in the instruction than in the child.

Even more helpful will be computer-adaptive assessment, in which the assessment responds to the individual student's answers; making the questions easier or harder in order to identify the upper and lower limits of that student's knowledge.

Innovation is opening these new dimensions of achievement

All this should make clear how many dimensions of achievement and assessment there are that need to be thought about; how many are not captured in the simplistic measures promoted by some in the policy discussion and so often parroted by the media.

Again—and this cannot be repeated too often—dramatic departures from the givens of the traditional . . . from the givens about achievement or from the givens of school generally . . . are not offered as 'the right way', 'the best way' for schools generally. *They are things to try on the 'innovation' side of the 'split screen'.* The idea is to let some schools move to competency-based progression, for example, if they wish; then let that approach spread if and as it proves effective.

Notice, now, how the major themes of this analysis begin to weave together.

Motivation increases achievement. If personalizing learning increases motivation, then we should have schools doing everything they can to personalize learning. If digital electronics can personalize learning, then expand the use of electronics. Personalization also elevates the importance of the teacher, the teacher being the only person in the school who knows the students as individuals.

So let's move next to ask: How, in schools on the innovation side of the 'split screen', might the digital electronics and the the teacher come together?

CHAPTER 8

Encourage 'Digital', To Personalize Learning

The pattern emerging from our discussion about motivation and achievement looks beyond 'batch processing' to the personalization of learning. So: How to create the conditions in which that can develop?

That takes us first to digital electronics: If 'digital' does facilitate personalization it will be important to find arrangements in the K–12 system that will speed the introduction of 'digital'.

Will education resist the introduction of electronics?

Lewis Perelman was ahead of his time in 1992 when he published *School's Out* about 'hyperlearning'. 'Re-forming', incrementally improving, school is a waste of time, he thought. Standards will become ceilings rather than floors. The right ideas for learning are more, better, faster, cheaper. Learning, he suggested, will bypass school.

In 1992 the implications of digital electronics were not so clear to others. The World Wide Web had been created only in 1991. 'Accountability' was becoming the strategy of choice. Adding standards was compatible with traditional school. 'Hyperlearning', too radical, was not admitted to the policy discussion.

Today it's clearer that a revolution is coming in the way people learn.

At the end of a talk about the way Google is disrupting 'old media'— newspapers, books, magazines, music publishing, advertising, the postal service—Ken Auletta, author of *Googled*, was asked: Is school old media? Of course, he said.

Every significant change in the handling of information, says Professor Lienhard, has produced a fundamental change in education. And today digital is rushing in.

'Online' is becoming one of the learning options. Education publications are filled with ads for new software to help students and teachers learn. Ads promote new hardware for interconnection. Books, sometimes themselves digital, describe the wonders ahead. Parents favor 'technology' and many of the students are skilled with electronics early. Their interest and capacity are significant assets.

An important question is how electronic devices are to be used. Will they be for the teacher or for the students? Will they standardize classroom teaching, or individualize learning? Will they reinforce or disrupt the givens of traditional school?

In mainline K-12 there is bound to be resistance to 'digital' disrupting its practice of age-grading or the technology of teacher instruction in conventional school. There will be an impulse to use digital the way new 'technology' was used when it appeared in other fields; to fit it into the current way of doing things. Motion picture cameras, for example, were initially used to film stage plays.[28]

Sometimes, too, those with interests vested in current practice try to erect barriers against the new-and-different. One Minnesota superintendent points to the regulations pushed by the textbook publishers. "I can put anything I want into a classroom if it's print on paper. If it's print on screen I'm required to get permission from the state department."

There does seem to be some concern about trying too hard too quickly to push 'digital' into the system organized on the industrial model, and some concern perhaps about the teachers perhaps going Luddite.

That might account for the eagerness to 'blend' digital into the traditional technology of teacher-instruction. The hope might be that

---

28. I remember wandering once into an empty math classroom in Humboldt High School in Saint Paul. On each student desk was a computer terminal. From each a wire led up to the teacher's desk. At her console the teacher could watch all the students' work. I thought: It was like this in my school—except that the teacher walked the aisles, looking down at the students' papers.

digital will then seem less threatening; that teachers will be reassured it will not too seriously disrupt their classroom. Downplaying 'online' and 'virtual' might also reassure the public there is no threat to its cherished perception of 'real school' as an adult with 25 students attentive to the teacher talking.[29]

The marketing strategy of the software industry might shape the new 'online' option. Whether 'digital' is marketed wholesale or retail will make a difference.

It seems hard to imagine state adoption of learning software, comparable to state adoption of textbooks. Yet the industry might press for at least *district*-wide adoption, to minimize the cost of sales. It could be a challenge to get big companies to want to sell school by school, classroom by classroom. Yet it is interesting to think about the huge flow of ideas for doing-better and to think what might happen were the teachers in America free to adopt what they thought best for their students.

To create a more receptive market it might make sense to move to the 'split screen' strategy, creating some schools in which teachers have incentives—reasons + opportunities—to personalize learning.

That probably can be done. Let's consider that possibility. It will take us to an interestingly different definition of 'technology'.

Technology is the way labor and capital are combined

When they hear 'technology' most people think about equipment and machinery: the robots in today's auto factories; the computers and stacks of blinking servers in a data center. They think about smartphones with their 'apps'.

That uses the term 'technology' for tangible things; for what economists call 'capital'. Some economists distinguish 'capital' from 'technology', defining technology as *the way capital and labor are combined.*

---

29. "A good teacher quiets the classroom", Bill Gates said, more than once, at the Education Commission of the States National Forum in Atlanta in 2012.

The classic example is the assembly line. Before Henry Ford and William Knudsen changed things a worker or a few workers built a whole automobile. In Ford's new factory each worker did one thing over and over as the cars came down the line. The new technology was not the machinery on the line: It was the assembly line; the different way of organizing work, the different way of combining capital and labor.

It is interesting to apply to education this definition of 'technology' as 'the way capital and labor are combined'.

The technology of traditional school has been whole-class teacher instruction. It was not capital-intensive: the 'capital' was not much more than books, blackboard, movie projector or TV set. It was *labor*-intensive. The 'labor' was expensive, even with a teacher handling 25 students and not highly paid. Today when school heavies-up the capital investment— as by giving the teacher an electronic board, by setting up a 'computer lab' by giving students iPads—that does not necessarily change the technology: It might simply be mechanizing the traditional technology of teacher-instruction.

• •

I went one day in the late '80s to an elementary school to watch a demonstration of some company's computer software.

The computer was not working right, and I'd always found it unsatisfying anyway to stand around watching someone else use a program. So I drifted out into the hall, just as a class of third-graders was filing into the computer lab next door.

I stood in the doorway, watching and listening. The lab attendant was standing close to me, but said nothing. The teacher was busy with the students.

The Apple II machines were on four rows of tables. The capacity of the central processor was limited, so the teacher had the rows of students take turns. Row A, hit this key. Then, Row B, hit this key. It went on like that, the teacher moving each row of students from key to key.

In front of me a little girl in Row D hit a key. The boy next to her leaned over and whispered, "You shouldn't have done that". Walking by Row D the teacher saw the girl had hit that key. Without saying a word she pulled the girl's chair back from the table. The little girl put her head down and her hands in her lap.

It went on. Row A, hit this key. Row B, hit this key. Pretty soon the teacher was back at Row D. She leaned down and said something in the little girl's ear. The girl nodded. The teacher pushed her chair back up to the table. Then continued: Row A, hit this key . . .

The lab attendant saw me taking this in. She seemed to feel she should make some comment. She stepped over to me and said, "This girl has been a problem. She likes to work ahead."

• •

It is possible, alternatively, to introduce digital electronics in a way that creates a new technology of personalized student learning, changing the way capital and labor are combined. Now with the enlargement of the capital investment—computers and software—the 'labor' changes: The teacher is no longer the only worker; the students now do more of the work, learning individually and helping other students (peer teaching). Teachers' work upgrades to planning, advising and evaluating.[30]

The question then becomes how the teachers—the workers in the old technology—will react as 'digital' arrives with its potential to create this new technology of learning.

Some will quickly see the need and the potential. But old ways die hard; the old technology of whole-group instruction might be slow to change. To get electronics accepted quickly it would help to make 'digital' work in the teachers' interest.

Think about the benefits of combining work and 'ownership'

To see how to do that, to see how to get the change to move faster on the innovation side of the 'split screen', consider the parallel in American

---

30. A meta-analysis at Stanford University in the early 1980s compared four interventions—longer day and year, smaller classes, computerization and peer-teaching—and found that peer teaching was the most effective, cost not considered. Cost considered, its appeal went off the charts. Yet in the discussions about improving achievement you almost never hear about peer teaching. Inquire in your district whether Spanish-speaking students are asked to help when the school teaches Spanish. Probably they aren't. Why not, for heaven's sake?

agriculture after about 1870 when farmers took up new machinery and new methods so rapidly.

That happened because—at least in the family-farm arrangement in the American Midwest and Great Plains—work and ownership were combined. In that arrangement farmers quickly realized that the new equipment and new practices made their work at the same time easier and more rewarding. So agriculture became vastly more productive and farmers became hugely better off.[31]

In manufacturing at that time, by contrast, work and ownership were separated. The rewards from new equipment and better practices in the factories went to the owners who employed the workers. Workers fearful of losing jobs sometimes tried to block the introduction of new machines and new methods. When that failed, they accepted the reality of change and organized to fight for a share of the productivity gains.

Test this workers-as-owners idea yourself. Ask your friends which of the two prior stages of the economy—the agricultural or the industrial—the new information age seems more like. See if most don't answer: Like agriculture.

Then ask: So why do we have education organized on the industrial model . . . making it difficult to introduce digital into traditional school?

Create schools in which teachers lead the learning

What if, instead, the 'family farm' arrangement were introduced into education, so that the school were the teachers' school and bringing in the new digital 'capital' was something teachers did in their own interest because it made their work easier, more successful, and perhaps also more profitable?

What if, in other words, the strategy for expanding the use of 'digital' were to create first, the conditions likely to encourage the take-up of digital?

---

31. As Norman Macrae, then its deputy editor, wrote in the *Economist* in 1984 after talking with Max Geldens of McKinsey.

Certainly it would be possible to try such a new arrangement on the innovation side of the 'split screen'; allowing the teachers, the workers, to make decisions as if they were owners.

It is more than a possibility, in truth. Both the chartered and the district sectors of public education today have schools in which teachers are able collegially to shape the program; have incentives to move to the new technology of personalized learning.

Efforts are under way, as well, to spread that arrangement.

CHAPTER 9

Open the Opportunity for Teachers To Work As Professionals in a Partnership

In school as traditionally arranged the teachers are not in a real sense professionals. Few things about traditional K–12 have been more firmly set than the assumption that teachers will be employees directed by a principal appointed by a board of education that decides what is to be taught and how students are to learn.

Teachers have not had the opportunity other white-collar professionals have had, to work in an arrangement in which they are trusted to know how to do what the client wants done. Richard Ingersoll's book asks in its title, *Who Controls Teachers' Work?* and makes clear that, whatever the answer, it is not 'teachers'.[32]

Conventional school reform thinks in terms of the traditional arrangement. Its advocates see teachers as unionized employees who resist change; bound to put their interests ahead of the public's and the students' interests. Persuaded that a good teacher is the most important factor in student learning, conventional reform wants to 'hold teachers accountable', wants to use student scores as the measure of teacher quality and to tie teacher compensation to scores as a way to encourage 'good teaching'.

It is a perfect example of thinking 'inside the box' about system arrangements and about the process of change. How can they not

---

32. Ingersoll, on the faculty of the graduate school of education at the University of Pennsylvania, researches changes in the American teacher cadre. *See* his website: www.gse.upenn.edu/faculty/ingersoll.

consider that the behavior of teachers and teacher unions might be a function of the public-bureau arrangement in which teachers work?

Moving away from the boss/worker arrangement for teachers would mean, first, stepping outside the assumption that education must be organized on the classic administrative-bureau model; decisions about the schools made centrally and 'professional issues' reserved to management.

Second, it would mean involving the teachers collegially in professional decisions at the school; arranging the schools so teachers work in something like the partnership arrangement common in most white-collar vocations: law, medicine, architecture, engineering, auditing, accounting, consulting.

Let's take the two dimensions of this redesign separately. Start with the delegation of authority to the working level.

Decisions are better when made close to the action

In 1988, when the idea of 'school-based decision-making' seemed to be taking hold among school principals, I was asked to discuss it at a meeting of superintendents.

Feeling it was not a good idea to go into that meeting alone, I asked Ron Hubbs to come with me. He had then just retired as CEO of The St. Paul Companies, where he had put through a decentralization of that big insurance firm.

In his quiet and persuasive way, he made the case against the traditional idea of central control.

> You just can't beat a decentralized system. It gets closest to the level where the action really is. Education should have an advantage in moving into it, because your locations and your people are already physically dispersed.
>
> Decentralization will not work unless you really delegate responsibility and authority. This means that the final decisions must be made at that lower level.

Persons in the software field use this photo in presentations all over the country to help people understand that to visualize personalized learning it's essential to step outside the concept of 'the class'. This is Minnesota New Country School, at Henderson MN; a grade 7-12 secondary that uses project-based learning and is run by a cooperative of teachers.

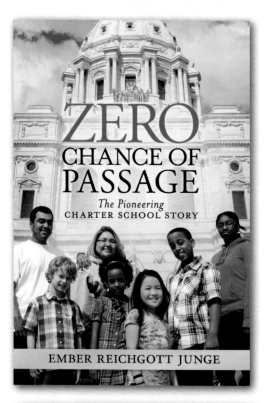

Zero Chance of Passage is the definitive account of the origins of chartering; Ember Reichgott Junge's account of her involvement as a state senator in Minnesota first in inter-district open enrollment and—beginning in 1988—her effort to add a chartered sector to public education. (A professor of political science would find it an outstanding case study of legislative process and politics.) Note especially the concluding Commentary by Louise Sundin, longtime president of the Minneapolis Federation of Teachers.

Amazon sells the book. Or order on zerochanceofpassage.com

For *Trusting Teachers* the authors examined about a dozen schools in which teachers "call the shots". Its findings provide the basis for the effort Education|Evolving is making to build awareness of the benefits of this model . . . and to explain what teachers change when, collegially, as professionals, they carry the authority and the accountability for student and school success.

For a copy, go to educationevolving.org. You'll see the cover of *Trusting Teachers*. A click there will show you where the book is available.

A Split Screen Strategy
Creating the Capacity for Teachers to Innovate

e|e education evolving

In 2012, as its thinking was clarifying about the split screen strategy, Education|Evolving produced this video of a teacher in a district near Saint Paul who individualized his third-grade classroom. It is a fascinating personal story . . . pedagogical story . . . policy story, summarized briefly in Chapter 5, page 51. To watch the video go to educationevolving.org/pai.

Creating the Capacity for Change, in 2004, saw the need for new dynamics to turn K-12 into a self-improving system. It proposed and argued for several of these: for choice, for chartering, for self-governed district schools. But 10 years ago we were only beginning to see the need to emphasize innovation in the new schools being created, chartered and district.

Copies are available from Education Week Press.

CREATING
How and Why Governors and
the CAPACITY
Legislatures Are Opening a
for CHANGE
New-Schools Sector in Public Education

TED KOLDERIE

teacher
powered
schools

@teacherpowered
Teacher-Powered Schools
www.teacherpowered.org

teacher-powered - *adjective*

1. collaboratively designed and implemented by teachers.

2. teachers having collective autonomy to make the decisions influencing the success of a school, project, or professional endeavor. As in, teacher-powered school or a teacher-powered evaluation program.

81% of Americans believe teachers have the know-how to make **schools** run better.

More than

70

teacher-powered schools
nationwide.

More than

9 in 10

Americans agree that
teachers should have more
authority in decision-making
in schools.

83% of Americans believe teachers have the know-how to make **classrooms** runs better.

Nearly **8 in 10** teachers believe teacher-powered schools could work.

Nearly **40%** of teachers believe having a greater voice in decision making would result in one of the biggest payoffs for student learning (second only to parental involvement).

60% of teachers believe the classroom and school settings are the biggest opportunities to impact positive change in K-12 education.

78% of teachers believe teacher-powered schools are a good idea; 85% of the American public agrees.

54% of teachers are very interested in working in a teacher-powered school.

1 in 5 teachers are ready to implement a teacher-powered school today.

CTQ CENTER FOR
TEACHING QUALITY
TEACHERS TRANSFORMING TEACHING

e e education|evolving

Source: *Teacher-Powered Schools: Generating Lasting Impact through Common Sense Innovation,* 2014.
View online at: http://www.teacherpowered.org/whitepaper

It is an innovation—arguably an invention—to introduce into education the 'partnership' arrangement common in most fields we call professional. Research done for Education|Evolving found support strikingly high for teachers having the authority to shape and run schools, programs or departments. It is further explained at www.teacherpowered.org and Chapter 9 explains the importance of this innovation for the effort to turn K-12 into a self-improving system.

Two things stand in way of this working: One is that the people who now have the authority may not let go of it. The other is that the people at lower levels may not want to accept it. And at the beginning, some of these people may not be strong enough to handle it. But as they grow (and they will grow) you can increase their responsibility.

The process is not as difficult as it might sound. You start at the top, by asking, "What is there that could be decided just as well by somebody else?" And then you keep working this question down the ladder. You really have to beware of the 'father knows best' attitude.

And it really does something for people. The executives are now essentially running businesses of their own. The company has confirmed their authority by making it very clear it will not let people dissatisfied with their decisions 'jump' over to the home office. Decisions are more rapid too. Most of our company's new executives are coming up out of this system.

It avoids the evils of bureaucracy. Business is afflicted with this, just like government. When decisions have to go to the top, it's not just a question of talking with the chief. His time is limited. So all kinds of other people up there . . . staff people . . . start to look at the question too.

I've never been convinced that more people make a better decision. It's okay to say to one individual, "You make the decision, and I'll live with it".

It will not be easy to move to that very different approach. Applying the idea to public education requires getting superintendents and boards to come to a different view about 'control'. This is not easy, because both are deeply into the idea of 'running the schools'.

Boards bring in a new superintendent to 'implement your vision'. Today, especially in America's large urban districts, a new superintendent's tenure is short. Big districts turn over their leadership every three to five years. Inevitably the new superintendents conclude they must move into a 'command' mode. Centralization follows, and standardization follows that.

And the challenge is not only to install such a new way of thinking. It is also to get it to last. Even were the current superintendent willing to think like Hubbs, a successor might arrive and wipe out the new arrangement. (Chapter 10 will consider how a state might act to create and protect a school-based arrangement.)

Still, it can be done—using the 'split screen' strategy; accepting that change starts small and spreads gradually. Remember: We are talking about innovations it is useful to try—not about a new scheme to install throughout K-12 comprehensively. The idea at this point is for some districts to try the kind of decentralization of decision-making Hubbs was describing. See how it works. Let it spread if it proves attractive to others.

Some superintendents will be willing. In some cities teachers will welcome it. Mike Strembitsky, a discontented teacher who almost accidentally became superintendent in Edmonton, Canada, implemented a delegated-authority arrangement there. He began with seven schools; let others come into the arrangement if they wished. By the time Mike retired, about 25 years later, the arrangement was city-wide.[33]

Next, let teachers collegially exercise that authority

Once there is a delegation of meaningful authority to the school the next step is to get that authority into the hands of teachers collegially.

That involves organizing a school—or a department of a high school, or a program in a district—as (loosely speaking) a partnership of the professional teachers.

'Partnership' is entirely conceivable as a way to organize teachers' work. It simply has not been education's tradition. The default arrangement in education—the boss/worker model, deep-rooted as it is in public and policy thinking—makes it hard to see and understand this organizational innovation.

---

33. This story is told at http://www.educationevolving.org/pdf/Strembitsky-Site-Management-In-Edmonton.pdf.

For years some individuals and organizations have been working to enlarge the professional role of teachers; sometimes calling their effort 'teacher leadership' and sometimes 'teacher professionalism'. Much of that discussion never gets 'outside the box', however. It talks of giving teachers (or suggests teachers take) larger roles in curriculum, pedagogy and district policy. All this is good. But while looking toward teachers getting these expanded professional roles *the effort still assumes the boss/ worker arrangement of school.*

The partnership idea steps outside that default arrangement: It inverts the pyramid; puts the professionals in charge; has the teachers responsible for the learning—and perhaps also doing the administration or having administrators working for them. In a freestanding school this has the considerable virtue of making it possible, when a problem appears, for the teachers to fix it quickly at the site.

The partnership idea contemplates the *dual*-leader model typical in other professional fields, where there is usually a top professional (chief of the medical staff, managing partner of a law firm) and a law-office or clinic administrator. That contrasts sharply with the single-leader model that has been traditional for schools.

In schools organized as partnerships the teachers sometimes assume the responsibility for both the learning program and for school operations.

The partnership idea can take a variety of organizational forms. Understanding begins with the simple principle of the teachers being— and being trusted to be—in charge of their professional work. Collegially, of course: This is not the concept of the individual teacher shutting the classroom door and doing whatever s/he pleases.

The idea can also be applied in a variety of ways. A partnership might cover a whole school. Teachers might also join to run a department in a big high school. Or a grade-level. Or a program across the whole district.[34]

---

34. Teachers were fascinated to hear Herb Morgenthaler, when manager of leased operations for Dayton-Hudson, explain how many departments in the store are not owned by the store, but are in the store on a lease. Teachers dove in with questions. In a few minutes they were looking around, saying: "We could organize a high school like this!" *See* http://www.educationevolving. org/pdf/Leased-Vs-Owned-Departments.pdf

Schools organized as partnerships do not work in theory: Conventional theory insists there cannot be a good school without 'a strong principal'. "Somebody has to be in charge", people in higher authority say. But schools in which teachers lead the learning do work—as partnerships do in other white-collar vocations.

The partnership innovation is now being tried

A professional arrangement for teachers' work is appearing and is now being tested in schools around America and is producing encouraging results.

An important beginning was in a small community about an hour southwest of the Twin Cities area in Minnesota.

The state's 1991 chartering law said a school could organize as a nonprofit corporation or as a cooperative. Early, several persons wanting to start a high school were interested in the cooperative idea. They were advised to form the school as a nonprofit—and to form a cooperative separately as a vehicle for the teachers.

This was the model adopted for Minnesota New Country School in 1992 (see color insert). In 2000 Tom Vander Ark, the first executive director for education at the Bill & Melinda Gates Foundation, made them a grant to replicate the model. In the years since, New Country has become one of the most noticed schools in America, in some years attracting 400 visitors from around the country and around the world.

The partnership idea has begun to spread.

A decade ago, Joe Graba with Education|Evolving began urging those he met in the Teacher Union Reform Network (TURN) to think strategically about their situation; to consider that the professional-partnership model might help them out of the corner into which they have been backed by the pressures for accountability (About which more below.)

Concurrently, on behalf of Education|Evolving, Kim Farris-Berg and Edward Dirkswager were finding schools organized and operating with "teachers calling the shots", and were looking at a dozen or so of the most fully 'teacher-powered' to see what changed when teachers came substantially to be able to control their work. Their book in 2013— *Trusting Teachers with School Success*—reported how significantly the teachers revised the approach to student learning.

Impressed by the response in TURN and to *Trusting Teachers*, Graba in 2013 advised Education|Evolving that the time was right to take the idea to teachers and the public across the country.

Education|Evolving retained Widmeyer Communications, which began by researching teacher and public opinion.

Not surprisingly, it found little awareness of the concept; of the partnership idea being applied to teachers.

With the concept explained, it found three-quarters of the teachers saying they thought schools or programs "collaboratively designed and implemented by teachers" a good idea. More than half the teachers said they would be interested in working in such a school, with one in five ready to join a 'teacher-powered' school today. The research found support for the idea among the general public higher still.

These are poll numbers that usually impress people in political life.

The Widmeyer results reinforced findings by Public Agenda ten years earlier. In that survey the Yankelovich firm had asked, "How interested would you be in working in a charter school run and managed by teachers themselves?" The question required teachers to affirm an interest in coming into the chartered sector in order to get to the 'run and managed by teachers' idea. Still, 58 percent of the teachers said they would be somewhat or very interested; two-thirds of the under-five-year teachers and half of the over-20-year teachers.

Education|Evolving and the Center for Teaching Quality are now working nationally to build awareness of, interest in, support for and use of the 'teacher-powered' idea. Interested teachers come together on www. teacherpowered.org and 'teacher ambassadors' are available to do lightweight consulting in cities where teachers would like to act.

'Teacher-powered' can address three problems in the system

Where teachers are trusted to lead the learning three things can happen. The new arrangement can:

- **Improve learning,** by eliciting from teachers that extra level of discretionary effort that will in turn motivate students.

The current policy discussion talks about 'better teaching'. But it usually assumes the current 'technology' of whole-class instruction; fails to ask, 'What's teaching?', so fails to consider how teachers should change, or might change learning with the arrival of digital electronics. In the new technology of personalized and project-based learning a new technology of learning can emerge.[35]

Teachers who in the partnership model accept responsibility for their school's performance immediately understand that the school's success will depend on what the students do. They see the key is to increase students' motivation. They adjust the learning program to maximize students' engagement.

Only the teachers can do this, because only the teachers know the students as individuals; understand their motivation and their aptitudes.

- **Attract and hold top-quality people** by making teaching a better job and a better career.

Objectively, teaching is not a great job and a great career today. "Candidly", Arley Gunderman—at one time president of the National Association of Elementary School Principals—would say, "My job is to motivate as much as I can, for as long as I can, people who are in essentially dead-end jobs."

Teaching is not truly a profession today. Most people want to be able to realize their potential, to have responsibility, to grow. So not being trusted to know how the job should be done, not being treated as a professional, is, Richard Ingersoll thinks, the principal reason teachers

---

35. The new technology of learning will change the concept of the 'highly-qualified teacher'. Dee Thomas, who for years led the project-based school at Henderson, MN, put it squarely: "A teacher who knows only one subject, no matter how well, is not a qualified teacher for our school."

leave. In some cities they today object strenuously to the way their work is being 'scripted' by the district central office.

Nor is 'teaching' a successful element of K–12 education today. The teaching force turns over rapidly, even good states losing half their new teachers in five years. Teaching draws today from the lower ranks of college students. Teachers complain that their training does not prepare them for the realities of the job.

Much of the criticism directed at teachers is probably unfair. Most are probably as good as any; dedicated and hard-working people trapped in a bad system. There is a great deal of talk today about getting 'better teachers'. Yet arguably the 'quality' problem lies in the job; the answer is to make teaching a better job and career.

Some look toward better pay as the way to attract top candidates into teaching. Ingersoll explains the fundamental: *Education would have to outbid all the other occupations that want these people*, and realistically it cannot do that. The compensation it *can* offer is the satisfaction that comes from a professional job and career.

Simply put: How can it not be obvious that the way to get 'better people' into teaching is to make teaching a better job for its people?

Our country could, indeed, be getting more from its teachers. But not by making teaching a less attractive job and a less attractive career.

The new innovation sector can make teaching a better job and career—by opening opportunities for teachers at last to work as professionals. And can let that model evolve and spread as rapidly as possible.

- **Make accountability work** for both teachers and the public, by aligning it appropriately with authority.

The deal the country has had with its teachers is roughly this: 'We don't-give-you professional authority, and in return you don't-give-us accountability'. That was not a great arrangement, but for years it provided a stable relationship with America's teachers.

Now conventional school reform wants to change that deal. It insists teachers *are* to be held accountable for student success—while still not given professional authority.

Asking teachers to accept accountability for what they do not control is a formula for trouble. Teachers, like most reasonable people, balk at that; say with some justice that if boards and superintendents want to keep the authority over what's taught and how it's taught, then boards and superintendents should be the ones accountable.

Boards and superintendents decline the honor: Few of them resign when student learning does not improve. They say in effect: 'You're the ones teaching the students; you're the ones responsible.'

The effect is to leave authority and responsibility misaligned—always a bad practice.

Teachers might not prevail in this debate but, disaffected, they do have the option to quit. Ingersoll's studies suggest that is what they now do: Not long ago the modal teacher was in his/her 15th year of work; today the modal teacher is in her first year of work.

Within the management/labor framework, in short, the effort to improve teaching by toughening accountability is not going well.

What we have in this question about 'teacher quality' is another example of individual and organizational behavior being shaped by the incentives in the system design.

The sensible approach is to redesign the incentive structure, bringing authority and accountability together by internalizing the responsibility for teacher quality and accountability within the teacher professional group. *If teachers can control what matters for student and school success teachers will accept accountability for student and school success.*

If in addition teachers were capitated—given the amount spent in their school (or department or program), given the authority to arrange the learning, and allowed to keep what they did not need to spend—there might be monetary rewards as well.[36]

---

36. A group of teachers was asked one evening to assume they could design the math program for their middle school, could have the money the school spends on math, could keep for the program or as personal income what they did not need to spend. 'What would begin to happen?' was the question. The teachers said: 'We'd get students going as fast as they could go. We'd get parents helping at the home end. We'd take a look at computer electronics. We'd get students helping other students.'

That realignment of authority and accountability would be good for the public as well as for the teachers. It is likely to improve the teacher cadre and can relieve what threatens to become a difficult and dangerous conflict with teachers and their unions.

Can it be done?

Certainly it can be tried. In both chartered and district schools it *is* being tried. And in these schools the 'teacher-powered' approach appears to work. The arrangement can be extended and so, yes, it can conceivably be done.

It will require district management gradually to change its role; to move away from its traditional insistence on 'running the schools'. But this, too, can happen—even if gradually.

Boards and superintendents will then increasingly be overseeing the performance of organizations they do not directly own or control. They will be essentially managing performance agreements; managing for results.

That is a shift boards might want to make in any event. It is time to change a losing game, scaling back their large central offices and delegating authority to schools and teachers.

It is time to see if it is not better to be managing agreements—especially where the parties on the 'school' side of the agreement can be entities organized and operated on a professional model by teachers.

PART THREE

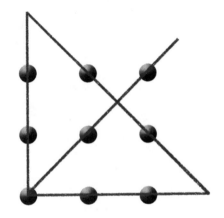

IMPLEMENTING

CHAPTER 10

The States Hold the Key to Implementing the 'Split Screen' Strategy

We come back now to the policy question: How to generate a climate of encouragement for innovation in the approach to learning and in the organization of school?

Let's say some states are moved to accept the 'split screen' strategy; to want real innovation. What does state policy do, to produce schools that step outside the givens?

Start by recognizing that state policy leadership cannot itself 'do' innovation. The system exists in state law, but the state neither creates nor controls the schools. Education law provides for local citizens to organize districts that create and run the schools.[37] A local board of education appears, usually (though not always) elected. The board appoints its own officials. The culture of 'local control' remains strong; districts resist state 'mandates'.

The job for the state, then, is to find a way to cause the districts to do what it cannot make them do. The way to do that is to create that 'climate of encouragement' for innovation.

---

37. Perhaps the principal distinguishing feature of public education in America is the delegation of this function to an independent special district, its members usually elected with no function other than, as they see it, "to run the schools".

First the state must organize itself for innovation

A state serious about encouraging innovation will have to make sure, first, that it is itself oriented to innovation. At the moment it probably is not.

K–12 education is overseen by 'the state education agency'—usually a department of state government, its head sometimes named by the governor, sometimes selected by the state board of education and sometimes elected. The state agency administers the law; writes and enforces rules. Today these entities probably do less than in the past to advise and support district learning programs. Like other bureaucracies, they work to get people to follow the rules; have difficulty with people seeking exceptions to the rules. The state agency is not often the source of innovative ideas for system change.[38]

When states opened the way for the chartered sector to emerge most simply fitted it—different as it is—into the existing state-level structure. The result has been that the state agency has been treating the chartered schools and their authorizers as entities to be regulated.

A state serious about innovation and about the 'split screen' strategy will need to tell the Department of Education to go on working with the traditional district schools, and to designate another existing entity or create some new entity, comfortable with innovation, to oversee the new sector.

Once the state itself is organized for 'different', leadership can then think about how to develop its innovative sector.

Revitalizing chartering is perhaps the best approach

With all its problems, chartering is probably still the best platform on which to develop the autonomous schools able to do-different.

Chartering has survived. Often, the new-and-different does not. When education's associations and their lobbyists cannot water-down

---

38. As Professor Tim Mazzoni of the University of Minnesota repeatedly reported from his research.

proposed legislation into a form they can approve, so have to deal with legislation of which they disapprove, they normally find ways to make the new legislation 'unworkable' and in time to get it quietly repealed.[39]

Despite the efforts to cripple it, chartering has remained. States could now refresh their chartering legislation, removing the regulations that have obscured the original concept of a deregulated sector. They could also push authorizers to solicit proposals for schools that will be new and different.

It is good to have multiple authorizers, with different approaches. One interesting variant appeared in Minnesota in 2009: the 'single purpose' authorizer. There are now four of these nonprofits—created new, deriving their authority from approval by the commissioner—able to devote their full attention to soliciting proposals, reviewing proposals, acting on proposals and overseeing the performance of the schools they approve.

IQS—Innovative Quality Schools—is a good example. It is proactive with its requests and seeks proposals for age-3/grade-3 schools, for schools that knit together high school and college and for secondary schools that offer technical as well as academic education.[40]

At the moment, unfortunately, the idea of strengthening innovation in the chartered sector runs against the effort of those now most prominently speaking for the sector. So—on the theory about never putting all the eggs in one basket—states should also look for other ways to encourage schools to step outside the traditional givens.

---

39. Randy Quinn, head of the Colorado Association of School Boards, was a fascinating exception. The CASB tried, but failed, to stop the chartering legislation in 1993. The following August he wrote in the association magazine that chartering could be, for boards, "a blessing in disguise"; letting boards become "a purchaser of education services". Asked, he said: "I began to see it during the legislative debate."

40. IQS describes itself and its operation in Appendix Two.

One alternative is to have the mayor take control

Some states have tried turning a city's schools over to the mayor; especially in large (mainly eastern) cities, some of which never had separately-elected boards of education. When mayor of New York City Michael Bloomberg went to Albany to get authority over the city schools and then began aggressively to develop a chartered sector.

It would be interesting to see a state try making public education a function of general local—municipal or county—government.[41] Something like that is happening with 'mayoral control', though this model is particularly identified with the notion of the elected municipal executive being personally in charge.

As has been clear in New York City, a program of change and innovation introduced by one mayor can be reversed by the next. This swinging with the political winds—as mayors emphasize and then de-emphasize chartering; centralize and then decentralize management—makes mayoral control seem a questionable arrangement.

Even were mayoral control found to be a good idea there are bound to be cities in which mayors would not seek to be in charge. So again: An interested state should keep looking for other possible arrangements.

Another is to try a smarter approach to 'state takeover'

Disappointed and frustrated by local performance, some states began moving in the 1980s to take control of districts plagued by low student performance, bad economics or corruption. New Jersey took control of Jersey City, then Newark and Paterson. Elsewhere, later, Detroit was taken over by the State of Michigan; as were Washington's schools, Congress acting as legislature for the District of Columbia.

---

41. In Finland, for example, the municipal government is responsible for public education along with public works, public safety, etc. Why people so commonly compare education here to education in states like Finland, without noting the fundamental difference in the governance arrangement, is a mystery.

Asked what 'takeover' meant in Newark, a key New Jersey official said: "We sent in four people". When I asked a few years later how it was going, he said: "Before, it was their guy. Now, it's our guy."

Probably takeover was not a winning idea. "When the state takes over", the New Jersey official said, "there is nobody left to be critical."

That early form of takeover displaced local representation, and predictably political pressures soon appeared for the state to return the district to local control—which many did, for better or perhaps for worse. As of this writing Detroit appears on its way back to the elected-local-board arrangement. Perhaps Newark, as well.

More recently a different version of 'takeover' has appeared—as in the Achievement School District (ASD) in Tennessee. Here the concept is to take over not the district but only the district's 'low-performing' schools: building, students, staff, management. The schools are reconstituted and put into chartered status or out to contract.

Chris Barbic, superintendent of the ASD, had, as of 2014, about 80 schools—most of them in Memphis and most of them elementaries—overseen by a 'district office' with about 40 employees.[42]

Intervening to fix failure can hardly be faulted. Still, that is essentially remediation. Better, probably, would be a 'prevention' strategy calculated to produce success in all districts.

A state can try enabling legislation for 'innovation districts'

Sometimes a state turns to legislation that authorizes and hopefully encourages districts to do what the state would like to see done.

Sometimes this legislation enables and encourages 'school-based management'. Sometimes it frees districts from state regulations that local officials say are holding back the district from doing-different.

Boards of education are usually happy to accept enabling authority so long as they are not required to use it. Given greater flexibility, some

---

42. By contrast, as Barbic discovered on a visit, Minneapolis with about 70 schools had about 600 people in its central office.

districts do use it. Where there is a progressive superintendent and where the board is cooperative, some significant things might be tried.

But as with mayoral control, the delegation of authority to schools is at risk for a change in district policy, in the superintendency or in the control of the board.[43] Again, too, not every district will use the authority granted.

So, is there anything else states might do to get districts moving to the 'split screen' strategy? Something still more radical, perhaps? Something that might more effectively drive the authority to do-different down to the school level and empower teachers?

There is.

The state might set up procedures for 'divestiture'

Governors and legislatures could act as decisively now as they did in the 1990s when—realizing that, like Zeus, they had the power to throw a lightning bolt—they created the chartered sector.

Administrators at the state level often talk as if they can do nothing unless given control or the power to command. Legislators think differently. They might not be able to command the districts, but they do have the power to change the system arrangements in ways that will cause districts to behave differently.[44]

Call this idea *divestiture*.[45]

State law has structured districts in a way that puts board members squarely in a conflict of interest; charged to get the best possible educa-

---

43. In Milwaukee, Bill Andrekopoulos, when superintendent, encouraged perhaps a dozen teacher-cooperative schools. His successor, more a centralist, reversed that arrangement wherever possible.

44. Arguably, they have a duty to do so. I remember saying to a group of state legislators at the Harvard Graduate School of Education in 1993 that the problems in K–12 are not the boards' fault, not the teachers' fault, not the unions' fault. "They're your fault. The boards and teachers and unions did not make the system. The legislature made this system. It's up to the legislature to remake it, because only the legislature can remake it."

45. Most of what follows is drawn from the 1990 memo. It is suggested here not by way of recommending a general system change but simply as another institutional innovation that a state might try.

tion for the children of the community yet charged at the same time to run the operating organization. Rather than searching widely for the best possible schools, the board puts the children into an organization it owns and runs and in which its members serve as the officers and directors. It is a self-dealing arrangement; an invitation to problems.

Divestiture would remove the board from its operating role, requiring it to bring in 'somebody else' to run the schools. It would drop the bureau model and in its place substitute performance agreements. Essentially it would implement Ray Budde's concept of the two-tier arrangement that has the policy body overseeing autonomous schools. It is the idea found today in the 'portfolio' model associated mainly with the Center on Reinventing Public Education.

No longer operating the schools, the board would have to focus on the policy questions: What are the learning needs? What do we want students to know and be able to do? Who will we bring in to do the work? How well is the job coming? What do we do if the job is going well or not well?

The superintendent would no longer be a 'school administrator'. The role of the urban superintendent would revert to the role of the old county superintendent of schools: *to oversee the quality of education in schools s/he does not own and run.*

In rough outline, a divestiture plan would:

- **Be selective.** The state might introduce divestiture only for districts of a certain size, or only for districts failing to make acceptable progress with learning, or only for those in its judgment showing inadequate interest in even trying to change.

- **Avoid creating disparities.** Occasionally the impulse to 'reduce the bureaucracy' produces an effort to break up large urban districts. Such proposals inevitably fail: People object, correctly, that this would create rich and poor districts in the different neighborhoods of the city. It is possible, however, to break *down* a large city school organization without breaking it *up* geographically. Simply drop the notion that reducing scale on the operating side requires reducing scale also on the policy and financial side. The two can change scale separately. Reduce scale on the operating side; keep the policy decisions and taxing at the city or district scale.

- **Give the targeted district a chance first to draw the divestiture plan itself.** The legislation could give each selected district a year, say, to design and adopt an arrangement of its own design. Only if the local district did not act would a state plan be imposed. Given this choice, the selected district might well prefer to write its own plan.

- **Offer the targeted districts options.** Here are a few:

  - *The plan*—the district's own or the state's default plan— might spin off the entire 'school administration' into a single public operating corporation and have a sole-source contract between the board and its former 'school administration'.

  - *At the other extreme*, there might be a performance agreement separately with each school, creating 'a charter district'.

  - *As a middle way*, a board might line up its schools and count off by threes—might form a Gold group, a Silver group and a Bronze group—and have a performance agreement with each. Have the entities operating schools offer their programs district-wide so that in every part of the district parents would have choices. Each would also design its own operating arrangements. One might elect to centralize; another might delegate authority to its schools. One or more might prefer conventional instruction; others might choose nontraditional learning, personalized or project-based.

· ·

John Maas proposed essentially this idea of divestiture when executive director of the superintendents' association in Minnesota in the 1970s.

Influential legislators were pushing at the time for consolidation. Conventional consolidation, merging the district administrations as it created a larger entity for policy and fiscal purposes, was unhealthy for superintendents' careers.

Maas and key superintendents suggested: Consolidate only the policy side; retain the several existing operating organizations. For example, the four districts in north Ramsey County—Roseville, Mounds View, North St. Paul and White Bear Lake—might:

- Create a single jurisdiction with a stronger tax base and a single elected board.

- Leave the four existing operating administrations, each contracted to the new board.

- Have each of the four operate schools in all parts of the new consolidated district, giving parents in each neighborhood choice among different organizations with different approaches to learning.

· ·

A state might insist on a divestiture, giving the targeted district/s only the choice between writing their own plan and adopting the state plan.

If more deferential to local control, a state might make its divestiture plan subject to approval by voters in the district.

Or a state might put into law a process through which local citizens can design and approve some new arrangement for their schools. As an example: In 1947 Minnesota put into law two plans for municipal government, either of which could be put to the voters for approval, by the local council or, failing council action, by citizen petition. That law (urged by the secretary of the state league of municipalities) was quickly adopted by the suburban 'village councils'. It succeeded in getting competent front-line local government—the city manager form—into place just ahead of the Twin Cities' wave of postwar development.

Boards divested of their operating responsibilities would have substantially more influence over the learning program than they have today: to diversify it, to change it and to hold its operators accountable.

What will get the state to move?

Governors and legislators who see the need for system change and who understand the need to 'get the fundamentals right' might be willing to get districts to introduce incentives for innovation.

They will need political support. The experience with chartering— enacted by governors and legislators as a 'state capitol policy initiative' without broad-based support—is unlikely to be repeated. To get the states to push the districts, somebody will need to push the states.

CHAPTER 11

Might a Teacher Rebellion Tip the Politics?

Is it possible the teachers might lead this country out of the wilderness in which it has been wandering?

It is. There can be no assurances. But it is possible. And something of that sort is necessary. Sweet reason and persuasive argument about the importance of system redesign will not be enough. There will have to be some powerful interest pushing for change. And that just might be the teachers.

A system redesign is now very much in the interest of the teacher unions. There is a real chance that a bold move could win simultaneously both the improved education the public seeks and the professional status they have sought for their members—and so far have not been able to secure either through bargaining or through legislation.

So it is very much worth asking: *What if the teachers themselves were now to make the 'split screen' strategy their cause?*

Interest is clearly building in enlarging teacher roles

The way to start is to get decisions about how-to-teach into at least some schools and to get authority and responsibility over those professional issues placed with the teachers.

That is something the public and state policy leadership should support. After 30 years of betting on district management being able to do the job it is time to see what teachers can do. Nothing compels the country to go on endlessly doing what has not been working well so far.

This effort *would* come within the 'split screen' strategy, of course; schools delegated authority so that teachers can personalize learning for their students. States and districts that want to continue attacking the problem as one of performance can stay with their effort to tighten accountability within the traditional arrangements.

You can see interest building in what is conventionally termed 'teacher leadership'. *Education Week* did a wrap-up in early March 2015. Rick Hess brought out his book, *The Cage-Busting Teacher*. 'Teacher leadership' is now a continuing theme for the National Network of State Teachers of the Year. Both teacher unions have people working toward larger professional roles. At the NEA Leadership Conference in Anaheim, CA, at the end of February 2015, there were packed houses for sessions on teachers leading the learning.

Much if not most of this discussion stays carefully 'inside the box'; looks for ways to enlarge teacher roles within the framework of conventional school where teachers remain employees directed by an administrator assigned to implement a learning program set by district management.

The idea of 'teacher-powered' schools, programs and departments crosses the bridge to a fundamentally different arrangement in which the teachers as professionals are in charge of the learning and either do the administration or have the administrators working for them.

For the unions this is the way out of the accountability dilemma

Teachers and teacher unions have perhaps the largest stake in seeing the states arrange the system so autonomous schools can innovate and so teachers can have a professional career.

The pressure from conventional 'school reform' is making action urgent.

Fearful that efforts to tie compensation to student scores might succeed, the unions are working to block or to slow testing. That reinforces reformers' belief in the malign influence of the unions. So it might be a strategic mistake.

Teachers and their unions ought not to get on the wrong side of the 'accountability' question. Resisting the pressure for accountability, giving ground grudgingly and as slowly as possible, is costing them public and political support. It suggests that conventional school reform is correct that teachers and their unions are standing in the way of improvement.

The better response, the obvious move for the unions, is to propose that new deal that aligns accountability and authority.

The question is how teachers might engineer this settlement of the accountability issue.

What if teachers were to demand meaningful authority?

Teachers might simply push for the arrangement described in Chapter 9, for the delegation of authority to the school and, in the school, for their right to handle that authority.

Where there is an opportunity legislatively, teachers and their unions could push bills for 'site management' or for 'self-governed schools'.

Louise Sundin, for years president of the Minneapolis Federation of Teachers and on the executive committee of the American Federation of Teachers, has come to the view that if there will ever be schools that give teachers real professional roles, teachers will have to create them. She is not alone.[46]

A more aggressive move would be for teachers, in bargaining at the local level, to press for the authority to decide how teaching and learning should proceed in their school. Boards would resist, insisting the law

---

46. *See* her epilogue in *Zero Chance of Passage*, essentially her testimony to the Minnesota Senate in 2011 when supporting a bill needed to open the way for union leadership to create a 'single-purpose authorizer' in Minnesota's chartering program.

gives them control of such matters and that 'professional issues' are not bargainable issues.[47]

But in Saint Paul the Federation local did just that during the last bargaining round, winning among other things a provision for 'micro-bargaining' that allows an individual school to negotiate with the board for a delegation of authority to that school. This accepts the 'split screen' strategy: would start with a few schools; build success; expand gradually.[48]

This would, to be sure, represent a kind of 'civil disobedience'. But that is the way, is it not, that much social change proceeds. Challenging the consensus, challenging even the law, works when the case for change is persuasive with the public.

Trusting teachers is an innovation that policy should try

For the unions this is the way out of the corner into which conventional school reform has backed them.

Teachers will have a strong case that teacher professionalism is in the public interest. They can show that 'teacher-powered' is the route to personalization, that personalization will improve student learning, that professional roles will attract quality people into teaching, that this is the preferable solution to the argument about accountability in K–12.

With a bold move, they might win their members control of professional issues and open the way to better learning. It should be win-win.

If the teachers do move toward this new arrangement—accepting accountability in return for professional authority—they might also use their considerable influence to push the states to support them as they test what can happen when teachers have professional roles in autonomous and accountable schools.

---

47. Sam Romer, when labor reporter for the *Minneapolis Tribune*, always advised: a bargainable issue is what either party insists on making a bargainable issue.

48. The then-president of the Saint Paul local, Mary Cathryn Ricker, has since been named executive vice president of the American Federation of Teachers.

CHAPTER 12

National Policy Should Help the States To Get the System Right

The role for national policy is to push the states to turn public education into a self-improving system. It is time at last for national policy to be strategic.

National policy will need to be an exercise in diplomacy

The system exists in state law; the national government cannot directly change state law. So success will require Washington to engage in diplomacy.

- Having reserved questions of system structure to themselves, the states could be moving to install arrangements that make education a self-improving system.

- They are constrained by resistance from a district sector more interested in preserving local control than in asking the legislature for system arrangements that would let its schools be more successful.

- To overcome these constraints the states will need to be pushed.

- National policy should do that pushing. But, diplomatically. Mandates and regulations won't get it done.

Our national government is right to be concerned about the need to raise the level of knowledge and skills in young people and to improve the schools they attend. It must, however, be strategic, accepting that its effective role will be to *cause* improvement. Trying to regulate and mandate is not the way to get action from entities the national government does not own and does not control, and whose leadership it does not appoint.

To say the national government must turn to the states for system-redesign is not to surrender to the ideology of 'states' rights'. It is simply to acknowledge that, as a practical matter, it makes more sense to work through the bodies that in fact have the power to redesign the system.

It is also to acknowledge that the national government has other pressing responsibilities that are its alone: foreign policy, defense, homeland security, the national economy.

Not every 'national problem' is one for the national government

The national government's involvement in elementary/secondary education began small and has grown gradually—and steadily.

Initially its role was limited: establishing and financing particular programs to help particular groups; up to World War II, the most significant probably the program for vocational education begun in 1917.

After World War II Congress began working to improve equity: helping the poor, requiring schooling for children with special needs, ensuring civil rights.

Only in the 1980s, as the schools in America came under growing criticism, did it turn to an effort to improve learning and the quality of the schools generally . . . the idea developing that 'education' is a national problem.

It is, and it isn't.

Clearly it is important for America to raise the level of knowledge and skills in its population. Still, 'America' does not have schools. Ask in Europe how well 'Europe's schools' are performing, and people will politely explain that 'Europe' does not have schools: Finland has schools,

Germany has schools, England has schools. In the same sense: Massachusetts has schools, Texas has schools, California has schools.

Despite the obvious differences between a continent and a country, people continue to compare America with the nation-states of Europe—and, astonishingly, even with cities; Hong Kong or Shanghai.

Washington politics turns almost any problem appearing across America into 'a national problem'. It assumes a national problem must have a 'national solution'. It concludes that a national solution means action by the national government.

On the question whether national action is a good and successful idea the experience in the 1960s with urban policy might be instructive.

Tying requirements to federal aid failed as an urban policy

As suburbs grew around the old central cities after World War II a new metropolitan problem was appearing all across America. No one was in charge of balancing the development on the suburban fringe with the redevelopment of the urban core. Disparity—and conflict—was increasing among the municipalities. This 'fragmentation' and the need for planning was declared a national problem.

The urban system, like the education system, is made up of institutions set in state law, with most of its elements owned and operated by local (occasionally state) entities: housing and building codes, zoning, streets and freeways, transit, parks, land-use controls, water and sewer systems, the property tax system and the structure and financing of local government.

Still, the national government moved to take charge.

A new department—Housing and Urban Development—was created. In 1966 Congress accepted the administration's notion that the solution lay in metropolitan planning. Each region would be required to create a regional council; each council would be required to develop a regional plan. Federal aid for urban facilities would go only to projects consistent with the regional plan. From this, the nation was assured, orderly metropolitan development would proceed.

What in fact proceeded was nothing of the sort.

Washington politics ensured that members of the regional councils were to be sitting officials of city and county governments. No way were these officials going to find an application from their locality inconsistent with the regional plan, or create a regional plan with which local applications would not be consistent. The councils became what David Walker of the Commission on Intergovernmental Relations called "paper mills", routinely approving everything submitted for review.

The whole apparatus was shut down by the administration that came into office in 1981. Today, the national government does not talk about having a 'national urban policy'.

In education, similarly, national policy has moved to take charge.

In 1979, at the president's urging, Congress created a new Department of Education. In 1983 the *Nation at Risk* report issued the call to action. In 1989, the first national summit—at Charlottesville, VA—moved to set national goals. By 2000, the polls were showing 'education' to be the public's top concern. Late in 2001 Congress enacted the president's campaign slogan about 'leaving no child behind'.

The states were to develop standards to ensure learning would improve. Requirements tied to federal aids would ensure state and local compliance. The national government was now to be, Christopher Cross wrote, the conductor of the orchestra. "State boards, legislators and governors must now follow the score."[49]

'The score' was the strategy of 'doing improvement': going directly after the visible low performance; adding standards and accountability in an effort to raise performance within the traditional givens of system and school. There was little interest in system redesign. (In his book Cross devotes two paragraphs to chartering.)

The administration that came into office in 2009 instituted its "Race to the Top"; set up an Office of Innovation and Improvement. Most of its effort was, however, about replication. Again, national strategy took the form of attaching requirements to money; assumed the states would never refuse the money, so would accept any rules, regulations

---

49. See *Political Education: National Policy Comes of Age*, Chapter 9; 2004.

or mandates tied to it. Most recently has come the effort to get back to rigorous standards; to establish the new 'Common Core' national standards and assessments.

A theory might be developing that, though education exists in state law, the national government can change the system with aggressive use of the 'equal protection clause of the Fourteenth Amendment to the Constitution. But that would be essentially telling the states what they may *not* do. Better, probably, to take a positive approach.

Activate state legislation to introduce the 'split screen'

Perhaps in time the improvement-only strategy will take hold.

But perhaps it will not. Like the effort earlier at national urban policy, the effort now with national education policy might fail . . . officials producing prescriptions that say 'must' and regulations that say 'may not' until the effort collapses of its own weight. In 2013, the Senate committee handling education produced a bill 1,000 pages long.

There is another strategy available.

The national government could hedge the effort at improvement-within-existing-arrangements by working at the same time to persuade states to create arrangements that let schools and teachers try new forms of organization and new approaches to learning.

Moving to this 'split screen' strategy would have the national government at last being strategic; at last 'getting the fundamentals right' by creating 'conditions' that encourage innovation.

The national government would have 50 different governors and legislatures to work with; 50 opportunities for its diplomacy to show how to get the system right.

It is interesting to think how differently a national administration might approach the states if it did see the challenge essentially as one of diplomacy. And to think how differently the states might respond.[50]

---

50. I suggested in *Creating the Capacity for Change*, in 2004, that it might make sense to transfer education policy to a domestic equivalent of the Department of State.

The president should activate the process of state lawmaking

It is possible to lead effectively without having the power to command. With skillful diplomacy, and using the 'bully pulpit' to shape public opinion, a president could be hugely effective.

All through his time in office, President Clinton gave remarkable support to the effort to introduce chartering into state law. In this he was implementing the centrist political strategy—a combination of public-school choice and chartering, in between conventional improvement and vouchers—that Will Marshall had shaped in 1992 when working up the policy book the Democratic Leadership Council produced for the incoming administration.[51]

Beyond the speeches and statements, a president could act directly to activate the process of state lawmaking, speaking directly to the legislatures of the states in a way presidents almost never have.

Nothing in the Constitution limits a president to speaking only to the Congress; nothing prevents a president from making proposals or presenting requests to the legislatures of the states.

A president could go to an individual state or to any number of them, and to the Education Commission of the States, the Council of State Governments, the National Conference of State Legislatures, the National Governors Association and perhaps to the Council of Chief State School Officers.

Why would a president concerned about so important a problem as public education *not* want to be working to activate the legislative bodies that have the capacity to turn K–12 into a self-improving system?

---

51. See *Mandate for Change*. Also, Ember Reichgott Junge's account in Chapter 30 of *Zero Chance of Passage*.

PART FOUR

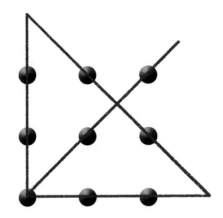

THE CHALLENGE

CHAPTER 13

It Is Time To Be Practical

It is not practical to work only on improving the performance of districts, schools, teachers and students within the traditional arrangements; trying endlessly to drive improvement into an inert system.

It is good to make the existing schools better. But—beyond being an unacceptable gamble with the public interest—betting all the chips on improvement-only is not practical. Nor is it practical to think of engineering a comprehensive transformation from the system we have into something dramatically different.

So how, then? What *will* turn K–12 into a system able to produce schools in which young people learn well?

The 'split screen' is the practical strategy

The effort has to be to convert K–12 from a static into a self-improving system. For this, there really is no alternative to the 'split screen' strategy of innovation-based systemic reform.

Start at the top.

The national government should be working with the states to continue improving existing schools within the traditional arrangements while at the same time pushing them to create a 'climate of encouragement' that allows and encourages schools and teachers to move outside the traditional givens.

This is 'getting the fundamentals right'. It is creating 'the conditions' that enable those at the working level to find alternatives to the traditional givens of school and learning. It steps around the impossible strategy of 'comprehensive transformation'.

Open to innovation and encouraging successful practices to spread, it is the way successful systems change. It can make K–12 at last a self-improving system.

'This is not a drill': Conventional school really is at risk

Being practical also means accepting that the future offers no assurance learning can be contained within the institution of school. If the K–12 system does not move to innovate, the new approaches to learning will sweep around it. The perspective of Richard Elmore of the Harvard Graduate School of Education is important. Learning, he believes, is now moving faster outside school than within it.[52]

The potential for this bypass is as simple as ABC. Already we can see its three elements developing: (a) ways for people to learn, (b) some entity to assess and validate what they've learned, and (c) a willingness to accept those validations on the part of the organizations or institutions the students want to enter next.

Disruption does sometimes come from an unexpected direction. The recording industry had long focused on new kinds of music and new ways of making music. MP3, which disrupted the industry, came as an innovation in *the distribution of* music. The transportation industry had focused on innovations with the automobile. Uber and the computers now disrupting this industry are innovations with *the driving of* automobiles.

Much of the discussion about innovation in education has focused on new ways of teaching and learning. It might find the disruption occurring instead in *the validation of* learning; with entrepreneurs offering new

---

52. See Jal Mehta, *The Futures of School Reform*, Chapter 7.

and much broader ways to assess what young people know and are able to do.

'School' assesses for what it has been teaching, focuses on the *exit* from high school and offers tests, transcript and the diploma as validation.

An 'outside' validation could—probably would—focus on *entrance*. That is, would assess for the full range of skills and knowledge young people have acquired, wherever acquired; would tell the organizations to which young people seek admission far more about their capabilities and their readiness than the organization can learn from test, transcript and diploma.

That kind of innovation at the point of assessment and validation would open to all manner of 'learning organizations' and learning experiences; would surely generate pressure on K-12 to broaden both its program of learning and its concept of achievement.

Nothing about the bypass would protect the equity principles of public education. But protests on that score would not stop its happening. Over time public education could drift down toward the status of public transit; continuing to operate, continuing to get substantial financing, continuing to have a high place in public affection—but declining in patronage as most everyone with the resources to do so leaves for a more personal and higher level of service.

Those who would most deplore such an outcome have the strongest reason to act now to help public education—both its district and its chartered sectors—to become a successful system able to preserve its principles:

- **Those who work in the institution.** They above all need to say to legislators: It is time, at last, to get beyond the traditional arrangements. We will not resist your doing that; we will help you do that. We will be accountable for student and school success if we can control what matters for student and school success.

- **Those outside who equate public education with 'the district'.** There are some who never accepted the idea of the state creating a new, second sector of public education; who believe education is public only where the schools are run by the city's elected local officials. Where that traditional arrangement is visibly not working well, their insistence on preserving the public-bureau arrangement—and its underlying principle that *there can be only one organization offering public education in a city no matter how large*—exposes these advocates to the charge that they care more about 'saving the system' than they do about saving the children. They should want the elected board of education to be effective; so should welcome the 'performance agreements' described in Chapter 10. The perspective of Paul Houston, when heading the American Association of School Administrators, might help. Public education, he said, is essentially a faith; a set of principles about access and equity and financing. "If we keep the faith", he said, "it will be OK to change the church. The church is not the faith."

'Torqued out'

When president of the Minnesota Education Association in the 1980s, Bob Astrup would sometimes describe conventional school, the conventional arrangement, as "torqued out".

He meant that as traditionally arranged the K–12 system is giving us the most it can—like an automobile that in its present gear can go no faster no matter how much gas you feed it. To go faster you have to shift into another gear.

This country needs to get more than it is from its schools and its young people. It *could* be getting more than it is, from both. But not with the kind of school we have, not with the system we have and not with the theory of change that we have.

'Shifting public education into another gear' means turning K-12 into a system that does innovation as well as improvement. It means shifting to the 'split screen' strategy so education can change and improve the way successful systems change and improve.

* * *

There is good reason to be hopeful. The appeal of schools that increasingly personalize learning has the potential to unite teachers, parents and—not least—young people into a powerful force for change.

APPENDIX ONE

The Rationale for an Innovation Sector

In Chapter 3 on chartering and in the discussion about the importance of system-structure in K-12 there are references to "The States Will Have To Withdraw the Exclusive", the paper circulated in the summer of 1990. Here are its early pages. Its latter part contained the proposal that appears in Chapter 10 for 'divestiture'.

* * *

THE STATES WILL HAVE TO WITHDRAW THE EXCLUSIVE
Public Services Redesign Project — July 1990

Seven years after the Nation at Risk report this country still lacks a strategy for school improvement. We are serious about improvement. But we do not know how to make it happen.

In the first effort, following the **Nation At Risk** report in 1983, we tried several things. We tried demonstrations, in the hope that good practice would spread. We tried mandates. We tried money: Real spending per pupil rose again in the 1980s after having risen by a quarter during the 1970s. Basically we were trying to get better performance out of the existing schools. It was not a great success.

Out of it came the conclusion that, if student performance is to improve, the schools will have to be changed. More than this: radically changed.

And out of this conclusion has come the current effort at "re-structuring". Nobody quite knows exactly what it means. But at its core there is a fairly coherent (and in a sense radical) vision: districts with professional teachers in "site-managed" schools, assessed and rewarded for the progress of the school in improving what students know and are able to do. This idea now dominates the conventional policy discussion about system-change and school-improvement.

But it is only a vision. It is not a strategy for action.

Institutions do not welcome change, especially radical change. They need a reason to change. And "re-structuring" does not give the district a reason to change. It assumes, as Jack Frymier put it in 1969, that "altruism is an adequate motivational base for change." It expects that boards, superintendents and teachers will do things they find personally difficult and institutionally unnecessary because these things are important for the country and good for kids.

This is not very realistic.

There have been some successes. There are important demonstrations in many schools. A number of districts have "restructuring" contracts. There is now a state (Kentucky) in which the program will be tried statewide. All of these are widely reported. The media create the impression of a changing system.

But change is more than getting words on paper, in contract or in law. Change must get established. It must last. And it must spread. The concern is that even in the most-noted "restructuring districts" the implementation is proving — as the superintendent in Rochester NY, Peter McWalters, said recently - "damned hard". In some districts the educators do not want to use all the authority they are given. In others the changes made may now be slipping away. The much-praised re-structuring in East Harlem, in New York City, has been in real jeopardy. Strenuous efforts by its friends may save it. But how many such defensive battles can be fought and won? For how long?

Above all there is the problem of scale. This country has 40 million kids and 2.2 million teachers in 84,000 schools in 15,000 districts. The problems are general, and serious. The change has got to be systemic.

"Re-structuring" is simply not moving fast enough for the job that has to be done. Privately there is real anxiety among those most committed to the cause.

"Re-structuring" improves on the old prescription: higher salaries, smaller classes and better training. But as it stands it does not go to the heart of the problem. It is trying to persuade districts to change while accepting as given the arrangement of public education that makes it hard for them to change. This makes no basic sense. We need a new approach. We need to examine the givens of the arrangement, find what makes it so hard to change, and change *that*.

Why Education Resists Change

The critical given is the idea of districting itself. The state does not deal with schools; it deals with districts. Legally schools do not exist: Districts exist. The district is defined by its boundaries. These create an area in which there is one and only one organization offering public education, to whose schools the students who live in that area are assigned. Public education is organized as a pattern of territorial exclusive franchises.

That exclusive franchise is the heart of the problem.

- It means the state agrees the district will have the final decision about improvement. Governors and legislators like to talk as if they control improvement. They don't. They can propose and promise, plead and threaten. They can give money. They can issue orders. And often the districts do respond. But whether they do or not in the end is up to them. If the district does not give the students a good education the state does not send in another organization that will. It accepts the pace of improvement at which the district is able or willing to move.

- The state also agrees to accept whatever reasons the district has for its decision to change or not to change, even if those reasons have to do mainly with the private and personal interests of the adults involved, as they sometimes do.

- And the state agrees to accept those decisions and the reasons for them, whether or not the students learn. Within very broad limits the state assures the districts their material success — their existence, their students, their revenues, their security; everything except their annual increases — independent of the level of student success.

Nobody should wonder why in public education "the cards are stacked against innovation". An organization with that exclusive franchise feels no need to change.

David K. Cohen put it gently when he wrote in 1986 that education contains "weak incentives for the introduction of innovations that would cause internal stress". And proposals for radical change surely do cause internal stress. Change disrupts settled routines. It upsets people. It causes controversy. It threatens the real interests of powerful organizations.

As they consider proposals for change the superintendent, board, principal, union and teachers weigh the potential benefits to the kids against the risk of creating "internal stress". They want to help the kids. But upsetting people might cause controversy. It might produce a grievance. It might lose an election. It might cause a strike. It might damage a career.

The risks are real. There is nothing countervailing: nothing that requires kids' interests to be put first; nothing very bad that will happen if the decision is to say 'no'. As things stand a 'no' is the end of the matter: The principal who wants to change has nowhere else to go; the teacher has nowhere else to go; parents and students have nowhere else to go.

There is almost nothing anyone can change without getting someone else's permission. Yet almost everyone has the power to check everyone else.

And practically nothing depends on making the improvements for which the public is pressing: clear objectives, measurement of performance, new technology or better learning methods.

Unless something quite unusual happens the students and the revenues will be there anyway. Good educators tell their colleagues, "We have to change". But that is not true in any real sense. They do not have to.

The kids get what altruism, courage and the random appearance of exceptional individuals provide in the way of improvement — which is often a lot. But the system puts them second. The system puts adults first. As Albert Shanker told the Itasca Seminar in Minnesota in 1988: "This is a system that can take its customers for granted".

Why the State Will Have to Act

For a country serious about improvement this is an absurd arrangement. We can hardly expect the district to do the hard things involved in change if we guarantee it its success whether it does these things or not.

This unproductive situation is not the educators' doing. The system is not one they created. Many might like to see it changed. Ted Sizer remarks near the end of **Horace's Compromise** that "the people are better than the system". That's true. The people are as good as any. They are working in a bad system.

It is time to say this: Our system of public education is a bad system. It is terribly inequitable. It does not meet the nation's needs. It exploits teachers' altruism. It hurts kids.

We ought to change it. It is unproductive and unfair to put people under incentives that are not aligned with the mission they have been given to perform. That leads to blaming the people for failures that are the fault of the system . . . and we are now deeply into blaming people for the failures of public education. Parents blame teachers and administrators. Educators in response blame parents, and kids. It is all wrong. We should stop blaming people. We should fix the system.

We can do this. We do not have to take the system as given. The system is a policy-construct.

But to change it we will have to go beyond the district. "We can never turn around enough districts," ECS President Frank Newman said in a "Statehouse to Schoolhouse" discussion, "without changing the incentives in the system".

Changing incentives means providing reasons and opportunities for people to do in their own interest and on their own initiative the "stressful" things that change requires. Changing incentives in the system means re-structuring the environment in which districts live.

It means withdrawing their exclusive franchise.

Only the state can do this. The districting is in state law. The responsibility for action rests with the legislatures, and with the governors whose proposals often begin the legislative process.

The state's job is not to run the schools. The state's job is to provide a workable system for those who do. It owes boards, administrators and teachers — and the public — a system in which those who do change and improve are supported and rewarded, and in which those who do not are the ones put at risk.

Everywhere in this country the state is in default on that obligation.

* * *

APPENDIX TWO
Chartering as an R&D Sector

In urging the need for an R&D sector this book has at several points suggested that the chartered sector remains the most logical platform for state policy to use. Making the chartering laws effective for innovation will require the states, however, to build that function into the authorizers in the system, the entities that approve and oversee the new schools. Here is the way one such authorizer describes itself.

* * *

INNOVATIVE QUALITY SCHOOLS: OUR MISSION, VISION, GOALS AND ORGANIZATION

Introduction

Innovative Quality Schools (IQS) is a Minnesota Non-Profit Corporation, approved as an authorizer of chartered schools on December 1, 2010 as a "single purpose authorizer" under Minnesota law. The sole purpose of IQS is to authorize chartered schools in Minnesota.

Minnesota law makes it clear that chartered schools are a part of Minnesota's system of public education. IQS aims to be a model of chartered school authorizing excellence and serve as a model not only for the chartered sector of public education but the district sector as well.

While the authorizing process of IQS is challenging, it is also fair, forward-thinking and transparent. A key aspect of IQS is its search for innovation and redesigned models of schools and schooling that result in improved learning for the students.

IQS will annually publish a "Request for Proposals" and circulate that RFP around the world in an effort to attract the very best proposals from anywhere that create the best learning options for Minnesota students. The RFP not only will identify the models of schools which the IQS Board seeks to authorize but it will also leave open the option of applicants to submit other models of schools.

The schools authorized by IQS will not be required to use specific curriculum, learning program or instructional methods, but IQS will require that some aspect of the school be innovative. IQS will require a quality research process for determining the impact of this innovation so that it is credible and can be replicated and disseminated in national journals.

IQS sees chartering as the R&D sector of public education. The schools authorized by IQS will be required to perform at high standards which will be reflected in personalized student learning, parent and student satisfaction, teacher professional satisfaction, recognition of the schools success and by state and national acknowledgement of IQS as one of the nation's premier authorizers.

Mission of Innovative Quality Schools

- Authorize a variety of chartered schools in both urban and greater Minnesota

- Hold authorized schools accountable for achieving high standards as exemplified by each student being a successful learner prepared for the challenges and opportunities of the 21st century

- Pursue schools that foster innovation in public education.

Vision of Innovative Quality Schools

- To be a model of chartered school authorizing excellence in Minnesota and for the nation.

- The students attending IQS authorized schools will excel in student learning that is tailored to address their individual needs and aspirations.

- IQS schools will be a part of the research and development arm of public education and as such will actively be working on school and schooling redesign in one or more of the following: developing new models of schools and schooling including new instructional models; providing new models of governance; researching innovative forms of measuring outcomes which have validity and exploring new forms of accountability; identifying efficiencies in the use of resources including expanded use of the digital platform; and, provide for new professional opportunities for teachers.

Goals of Innovative Quality Schools

1. Through a rigorous authorizing process, Innovative Quality Schools will authorize up to 26 quality chartered schools that result in meeting the individual needs of the students served as defined in the authorizer/school contract.

2. All schools authorized by Innovative Quality Schools will include a focus on innovation in one or more aspects of their operation and will competently research and disseminate the results of that innovative practice(s).

3. Schools authorized by IQS will improve both by learning from each other as well as through the high level of expertise provided by the IQS Cadre of Professionals.

4. Innovative Quality Schools will be recognized as a model of authorizing excellence for Minnesota and the nation by disseminating the impact of its authorizing model and assisting others.

Schools authorized by IQS will have common values

Sharing the values of IQS is important for schools to be authorized by IQS. These values are communicated to assure that only high quality schools with missions aligned with these values are authorized. In order to ensure that the schools authorized by Innovative Quality Schools will provide outstanding learning environments for students which result in high levels of learning, they will be selected in part if they demonstrate commitment to the following values:

- The individual needs, aptitudes and aspirations of each learner are paramount. IQS believes that personalization is the vehicle around which learning ought to be organized.

- Learning at high levels is key for all students. While IQS believes that high levels of attainment are the purpose of 21st century schools, that does not mean that it is appropriate for each student to excel at the same things...at the same time...in the same place. IQS-authorized schools will offer students the opportunity to excel in their areas of interest.

- Innovation is evident in some aspect of the design of each school. IQS believes that the chartered sector is the research and design sector of public education and, as such, IQS will be an authorizer which fosters the development of new and different learning models. While some of these will not have a strong research base, each will be testing a hypothesis. These schools will be the incubators of new improvements for the future. All schools authorized will be required to have at least one aspect that is innovative and is being researched.

- A small, safe learning environment is provided for students where families are welcomed and cultures are valued. IQS believes that small learning environments are conducive to learning and that schools must be safe for the students in today's world where all students from the world's rich cultures are welcomed.

- Critical thinking, creativity and self directed learning are necessary learning outcomes. IQS believes that these results are key aspects of the new models of achievement and will encourage schools to address these features.

- Learning is recognized and validated wherever and whenever it occurs using new and different evaluation models and establishing new forms of accountability. IQS recognizes that in today's digital world, students are learning on-line and from their experiences in the community. While the school will not directly provide for all learning, the school will either validate learning directly or by accepting the validation of others.

- The primary purpose of assessment is to provide information used for improving instruction and learning. IQS recognizes the importance of formative assessment and encourages schools to use data to improve the learning for students.

- A collegial professional learning community is provided where shared decision-making is evident regardless of the leadership model at the school. IQS places a high priority on authorizing schools where professional teachers develop the schools in which they practice their profession.

- Students, staff and boards expect and value being held accountable for results. IQS believes that all involved in the learning process must value being held accountable for their work.

- Evaluation of student learning is based on the growth or value-added growth of individual students. IQS understands that in today's mobile world, schools can only be held accountable for the students they have had an opportunity to teach for a period of time. IQS also believes that the schools should be able to ascertain the added value of the learning which occurs that can be attributed to that school.

- These are specific to the purposes set in (the Minnesota chartering statute) Section 124D.10 Subd. 1.

IQS will authorize schools throughout Minnesota that are designed consistent with the above values, but will place special priority on those schools with a clear innovation aspect: in the leadership model for the school, the actual model of instructional design, the evaluation model, the professional opportunity provided for teachers or the financial efficiency of the school.

IQS Success as an Authorizer

IQS will judge itself as an authorizer based on the following performance indicators:

- IQS will authorize 26 schools by the end of FY 15;

- The students in schools authorized will meet the rigorous goals provided for in the contract with IQS and the schools will be operated in a quality manner;

- Because of the innovations being researched by IQS schools, new information will be provided to the education community about teaching, learning, assessment, leadership models, evaluation and schooling efficiency;

- IQS self-study and independent evaluations will conclude that IQS is implementing authorizing practices in a quality manner as provided for in the MDE approved authorizing process based on the Five Core Principles of Quality Authorizing (see below) and that IQS is functioning within its budget;

- Schools authorized report that IQS is fair and transparent in its authorizing practices and that they are improved schools because of IQS authorizing;

- IQS will be recognized by state and national organizations as an exemplary authorizer; and,

- MDE oversight identifies IQS as a competent authorizer with continued re-approval of IQS as an authorizer.

The Core Principles of IQS as an Authorizer

IQS has organized its authorizing organization and practices consistent with the following principles:

- *Agency Capacity and Infrastructure:* IQS creates organizational structures and commits the human and financial resources necessary for conducting its authorizing responsibilities effectively and efficiently;

- *Chartered School Application Process:* IQS implements a comprehensive application process that follows fair procedures and rigorous criteria resulting in charters granted only to those who demonstrate strong capacity for establishing and operating a quality school;

- *Performance Contracting:* IQS utilizes a transparent oversight process of the schools it authorizes by initiating practices of continuous evaluation and compliance monitoring which provide information that is useful to the school for its improvement purposes while ensuring the autonomy of the schools it authorizes; and,

- *Renewal Decision Making:* IQS designs and implements a transparent and rigorous process that relies on data and information from multiple sources to make merit-based renewal decisions.

IQS Organizational Model, Board of Directors and Leadership

Just as IQS places an emphasis on innovation in the schools it authorizes, the IQS organization also reflects a redesigned model. IQS has no employees nor does it have an office. The Board contracts with both management leadership as well as a cadre of professionals with expert-level competence to do the authorizing work.

- **The Board of Directors of IQS for 2015-2016:**

Dan Mott Esq., chair; David Johnson PhD, vice chair; Arnie Weimerskirch, secretary; Edward J. Dirkswager, Jr., treasurer; Kristen Anderson EdD, Craig Amundson DDS, Mary K. Boyd, Holly Marsh.

The Board of IQS contracts the IQS management leadership to an independent entity, StrategicTrec LLC. The partners of this organization are:

Thomas Tapper EdD, managing partner; Steven B. O'Conner EdD; Milo Cutter EdS. Each has extensive experience in Minnesota public education.

- **Contracted Professional Cadre:**

Drew Brennan PhD, Karen Cadigan PhD, Walter Enloe PhD, Karen Erickson, David Heistad PhD, Doug Marston PhD, Phil Moye PhD, Don Pascoe, Cheryl Reid, Jerry Robicheau PhD , Ron Simmons EdD and Tom Watkins PhD, Bob Wedl, Scott Wurdinger PhD and Liz Wynne.

Each has expertise in one or more of the following areas: program models, governance, performance evaluation and research methodologies, finance and operations.

APPENDIX THREE

A Few Suggestions about Money and Change

Once, 'money' was a principal strategy for change. The notion was that only when financing was increased was change possible. That idea has now faded. So 'money' is not part of the theory of action set out in this book; partly on the recognition that it can work more to suppress than to promote change.

Still, it might be useful to add a few notes here about changes in the financing of K-12 that might facilitate the development of a self-improving system. Some of the system changes, the institutional innovations, in public education do require adjustments in the system of school finance. And of course, changes in the financial arrangements—such as to introduce support for early-childhood education—would involve action by state policymakers.

* * *

1. Use common sense about the appeal for 'more'

The initial appeal from districts is often that change requires additional financing; that without more revenue, they cannot change. Clearly, those asked to provide the money need to understand how to respond to this appeal.

- **Never trade money for promises.** Business and civic organizations—even occasionally governors—often sign on to help pass a larger appropriation or a levy increase in return for a promise from the district(s), or the system, to improve school and learning. This is a bad mistake. Getting improvement in the schools is not like buying a house, where the buyer pushes a check across the table and the seller delivers a deed in return. Districts cannot deliver improvement immediately. Improvement takes time. So the district essentially gives you an IOU; the improvement to be delivered later. If later it is not delivered, you're out of luck, have no recourse. So, do not trade money for promises. If you negotiate for change and improvement, identify the specific actions to be taken that clearly will produce change and improvement, make sure those actions are taken, then commit to the financing.

- **Is it really important if the district won't pay for it itself?** A superintendent's standard approach is to say the district needs money in order to change and improve. That pitch is often made to foundations. When presented, foundations should ask the superintendent, "Is this important?" If the superintendent says, yes, it is important, then ask, "Is it *very* important?" If the answer to that is also 'yes', then ask, "Is it *very, very* important?" If the answer again is 'yes', then ask: "Now explain to me why, if it is that important, it isn't important enough for you to pay for yourself?"

- When and where **does money matter?** Distinguish between the things for which money matters and the things for which it does not. I remember Pam Costain, former chair of the Minneapolis Board of Education, being asked one day at a meeting of the discussion group on the Achievement Gap about the need for greater resources. "I'm a liberal Democrat", she said, "and I believe in public spending. But I have to tell you: the problems this district has are not the kind of problems that money solves".

2. Use money to leverage change

- Periodically, districts come to the public—have to get a vote of approval—to borrow for capital purposes or to raise their tax levy. These occasions present an opportunity for organizations in the local 'civic system' to use their influence to correct weaknesses in the district's proposal or to get the district to do things it would not do without some pressure. A classic case occurred when the Minneapolis schools went to the voters in 1962 for the first district building program since the 1920s. Looking at the board's proposal, a local policy group, the Citizens League, saw it was a rehabilitation program, a few new rooms on every building in town—essentially a proposal designed to secure votes for the bond issue. Also, Minneapolis at that time had five high schools in a strip across the city south of downtown. The League urged the board to design a *replacement* program: closing whole buildings, selling those sites, building new schools at new sites. The board declined, went ahead with the vote. The League took the issue to the public, urging a 'no' vote. The measure was defeated. At the League's suggestion, the board then brought in a team from Michigan State—which recommended a replacement program. The capital plan was redone and resubmitted and with the League's support was approved. When the urban troubles came a few years later Minneapolis was building the newest high schools in the oldest parts of the city.

- At other times, too, the League would condition its support on the board (or city council), committing itself *prior to the vote* that it would take this or that specific action. This kind of constructive pressure can be effective in a referendum.

- Governors might try something similar, something different from what they normally do, when districts—individually or as a class—sue the state. Sometimes there are 'adequacy' suits, alleging the state is not providing 'enough'. Sometimes there are 'equity' suits, alleging unfairness to one set of districts or another. The impulse of the state's lawyer, the attorney general, is to deny the complaint. An astute governor, when sued, might use the suit as an opportunity for change—at least in states where the constitution requires the state to provide a "thorough and efficient" system of public education. The plaintiffs of course have in mind money as their relief, and a court presented with no alternative will likely accept that premise. A smart *governor* might tell the attorney general instead to *admit the complaint*—not with respect to money but with respect to the design of the K–12 system. 'Efficient' means "capable of accomplishing the result intended". Show that the K–12 system, as traditionally structured, is incapable of accomplishing the result intended. Lay out for the court a new arrangement that will turn K–12 into an effective system, a self-improving system.

3. Use the state foundation formula to finance choice

When the legislature 'withdraws the exclusive', takes down the old public-utility model of K–12, a question arises how the money follows the student moving from his/her 'home' district to the new district of attendance. This has been a puzzle for many states because school finance is most everywhere a combination of district revenue and state revenue.

Too often, knowing that the financing is a combination of revenue raised by local taxes and revenue raised by state taxes, people think that each student must be some combination of the two: part gold and part green.

No; not necessarily. Think about that combination of state and local revenue this way:

- Our foundation program asks each district to pay a certain proportion of its wealth toward the cost of educating its children. Whatever that proportion, that uniform rate, raises in dollars—the amounts varying because of the differences in property valuation—the state will then pay the difference up to a level defined as full cost.

- This makes it possible to think of a box of students base-loaded with local dollars—all green, in effect—topped off with a layer (of whatever depth) of students fully state-paid, all gold.

- A student moving from District A to District B is then a student 'off the top of the box'—all gold. So when the student moves, the state deducts the full per-pupil amount from District A and sends that full amount to District B.

That approach, used in Minnesota to finance inter-district enrollment, was used to get revenue to the chartered public schools—with the exception of certain 'excess levy' revenues approved by local voters over and beyond the state-defined 'full cost'.

4. When discussing equity in financing, talk about schools

The equity issue is usually raised by districts, often in lawsuits (see #2 above), arguing that the amount of revenue they get is 'not fair'. Often this appeal rests on their argument that their students, in the district as a whole, are needier. Less discussed is the question about equity as between 'needier' and 'not-needier' schools *within the district.*

In 1971, when Minnesota became the only state to re-equalize education finance through the political process, the legislation provided a 40 percent additional weighting on the formula for students from AFDC families.

It was intended that this extra revenue would go to the schools that enrolled those students. In the event, the district kept the money, used it in other ways.

The reality is that senior—and therefore more expensive—teachers tend to accumulate in the schools with the less-disadvantaged children. The board pays salaries, so larger amounts go to those more-advantaged schools. If the district were to allocate revenue per-student, then—on the existing salary scale—the schools with the more-disadvantaged children would have more teachers and the more advantaged schools would have fewer.

The politics involved mean that tends not to happen. This is a real issue, however. Press it.

5. Work to introduce incentives to use money differently

Districts definitely are *revenue*-maximizers. Whatever the level of spending, the appeal is for 'more'. "*Invest in Our Children*", say the banners. "Money makes a difference", say the lawyers and policy advocates. To the question, 'How much?' there is never a clear response. People in Minnesota remember a lobbyist for one major K–12 association, asked to define 'enough', answering: "All you've got plus 10 percent". What drives expenditure is basically revenue available. As the head of another statewide K–12 association wrote in 2012, districts "spend all the money they can get their hands on".

For those who provide the money for the schools, elected officials and taxpayers, the goal must be to get out of this game. Their interest is in introducing incentives for districts and schools to make better use of the money they get.